Beyond TV
ACTIVITIES FOR USING
VIDEO WITH CHILDREN

Beyond TV
ACTIVITIES FOR USING VIDEO WITH CHILDREN

Martha Dewing

ABC-CLIO

Santa Barbara, California
Denver, Colorado
Oxford, England

Copyright © 1992 by Martha Dewing

All rights reserved. No part of this publication may be reproduced, stored in a retrieval system, or transmitted, in any form or by any means, electronic, mechanical, photocopying, recording, or otherwise, except for the inclusion of brief quotations in a review, without prior permission in writing from the publishers.

Parts of this book were previously published as follows: Chapter One appeared in *Video Rating Guide for Libraries* 1991 2(3); Chapter Three appeared in *Children's Video Report;* Chapters Four and Five appeared in *Encourage Media Literacy! 161 Activities Too Good To Miss for Ages 5–9;* Chapter Seven appeared in *LA Parent Magazine* and in *Children's Video Report.*

Library of Congress Cataloging-in-Publication Data
Dewing, Martha.
  Beyond TV : activities for using video with children / Martha Dewing.
    p.   cm.
  Includes bibliographical references and index.
  1. Video tape recorders and recording—Library applications.
2. Libraries—Special collections—Video recordings. 3. Libraries, Children's—Activity programs. 4. School libraries—Activity programs. 5. Audio-visual library service. 6. Video tapes in education. 7. Mass media and children.   I. Title.
Z692.V52D49 1992   027.62'5—dc20   91-40441

ISBN 0-87436-601-1

99 98 97 96 95 94 93 92   10 9 8 7 6 5 4 3 2 1

ABC-CLIO, Inc.
130 Cremona Drive, P.O. Box 1911
Santa Barbara, California 93116-1911

This book is printed on acid-free paper ∞ .
Manufactured in the United States of America

I absolutely believe in the idea that things children are exposed to are laying down patterns in their brains. And so you can't read early enough to a child, you can't talk early enough to a child, you can't love early enough for a child, you can't bring music early enough into a child's life—it becomes part of the patterning.

> Maurice Sendak
> *Children's Video Report*
> 1987 2(4)

Contents

Preface, xi
Acknowledgments, xv
Introduction, xvii

ONE **Guidelines for Building a Video Collection, 3**
Video in the Classroom, 4
Video and the Public Library, 4
Conceptualizing the Children's Collection, 5
Evaluating and Selecting Videos, 7

TWO **Using Video as a Catalyst for Thinking, 11**
Selecting Videos for Classroom Use, 11
Facilitating Children's Responses to Video, 12
After the Video: Facilitating Discussion, 13
The Importance of "Deep" Questioning, 16

THREE **Children's Media Needs by Age, 19**
Preschool, 19
Kindergarten through Third Grade, 20
Fourth through Sixth Grade, 24
Summary of Children's Media Needs by Age, 26

FOUR **Video Activities for Kindergarten through Third Grade, 29**
Understanding the Story, 29
    Story: Beginning, Middle, and End, 29
    Elements of a Story, 30

Stories and Visual Imagery, 32
Comparing Videos and Books, 33
Dramatization Activities, 34
Music and Movement, 35
Art Activities, 35

Understanding Video Production, 37
Video Elements, 37
Acting and Characterization, 37
Animation, 38
Costumes and Scenery, 39
Producing, 39
Scripting and Storyboarding, 40
Using a Video Camera, 41
Sound, 41
Special Effects, 42

Using Video To Build Skills and Knowledge, 43
Listening Skills, 43
Media Awareness, 44
Storytelling, 46
Science and Social Studies, 46
Thinking Skills, 47

And Just for Fun, 49

FIVE Video Activities for Fourth through Sixth Grade, 51

Understanding the Story, 51
Elements of a Story, 51

Understanding Video Production Techniques, 63
Acting, 64
Animation, 65
Camera Work, 66
Color versus Black-and-White Photography, 68
Costumes and Scenery, 69
Editing, 69
Production Values, 70
Scripting and Storyboarding, 70
Sound, 71
Special Effects, 72

Contents ix

  Special Technology, 73
  Using the VCR, 74
  Video Production Activities, 74

Using Video To Build Skills, Knowledge,
  and Understanding, 76
  Books and Video, 76
  Exploring Emotions, 77
  Exploring Values, 78
  Prejudice and Stereotypes, 78
  Language, Speaking, and Writing Skills, 78
  Media Awareness, 80
  Science and Social Studies, 84
  Thinking Skills, 84

SIX Connecting Activities with Specific Videos, 87

Using Video To Understand and Appreciate
  Language and Literature, 87
  Purpose: To Explore the Elements of a Story, 87
  Purpose: To Explore Character Development, 90
  Purpose: To Explore Journal Writing, 92
  Purpose: To Enjoy Words and Build Vocabulary, 93
  Purpose: To Explore the Concept of Evil in Characters, 94
  Purpose: To Understand Heroes/Heroines, 95
  Purpose: To Explore the Concept of Going on a Quest and How It Relates to Plot and Character Development, 96

Exploring and Understanding How Videos Portray
  and Evoke Emotions, 97
Using Video To Explore How Others Live, 98
Using Video To Understand Communication, 99
  Purpose: To Understand Other Forms of Communication, 99
  Purpose: To Learn about Closed Captions, 100

Using Video To Teach Critical Viewing, 102
  Purpose: To Understand the Power of the Message, 102

Learning To Evaluate Videos and Television, 103
Using Video To Practice Creating and Using an Outline, 103

Using Video for Research, 105
    Purpose: To Encourage Students To Use Video as an Additional Source of Information for Research Projects, 105

SEVEN   Helping Parents Cope with Video, 107
Regulating Children's Video Consumption, 109
The Value of Children's Video, 110
Deciding Which Tape To Choose, 112

APPENDIX A: Suggested Video Titles, 115
    Alphabetical List, 116
    Video Titles by Category, 141
APPENDIX B: Organizations, 159
    Distributors of Children's Video, 160
APPENDIX C: Print Resources, 163
    Specialty Publications, 163
    Books about Literature and Story, 163
    Books about Media, 167
    Books about Children and Child Development, 173

Glossary, 177
Index, 181

Preface

As an elementary school teacher in the 1970s and early 1980s, I was able to observe firsthand the impact that various media had on my students. Although television was an important part of their lives, we rarely discussed it in the classroom. Periodically, I overheard snippets of conversations about one program or another, but I paid little heed.

The term *video across the curriculum* had not yet been coined, but I knew the power of film and used it with each subject that I taught. Sea life, math concepts, Australia and the Aborigines, the lives of individuals such as Helen Keller and King Tut—whatever the specific curriculum was, I sought films to complement each subject and bring it to life for my students. My goals were to stimulate the children's curiosity and to increase their understanding of the material. I carefully selected films that enhanced the subject matter and were appropriate for the age group of my students.

Because the films were interesting and provided the right amount of challenge, the children became involved and were motivated to learn more. This led to insightful discussions. For example, after reading about Helen Keller's disabilities and learning how Annie Sullivan taught her to communicate, my classes of second graders were eager to see a film about these two inspirational people who had piqued their imaginations. They watched *The Miracle Worker* (MGM/UA, 1962) in three sittings of approximately 30 minutes each. (Research indicates that when children are shown a lengthy film or video in the classroom, they derive more benefit from several short viewing sessions than from one long one.) Time was provided for discussions both before and after each viewing. To say that the children were absorbed with the movie would be an understatement. They asked questions, talked about Helen among themselves, and role-played her as a child and as an adult. Those who had not already read a biography about her life did. Those who had done so sought out another or went on to read about other blind and deaf children. The power of the medium was evident.

When I decided to leave teaching in 1983, I knew that I wanted to focus on uses of film with children. The mass use of home video was then in its infancy. Seeing video's potential in the home and its power as a teaching tool, I began publishing the *Children's Video Report* in 1984, in order to ferret out good programming and to help people working with children to use the medium as a resource for learning. Since its inception, the newsletter has examined such topics and issues as fairy tales, the environment, animation, tolerance, and science fiction.

How This Book Is Organized

Chapter One of this volume offers guidelines and recommendations for consideration by those creating video collections in schools or libraries. Chapter Two contains practical tips for using video with children, along with suggestions for conducting classroom discussions in order to ensure that each child derives maximum benefit from the viewing experience.

Chapter Three describes how children of different ages are affected by visual imagery and stories. Using the tale of "The Three Little Pigs" as a model, the chapter examines different adaptations of this tale and explains why an adaptation that works for one age group may not work for another.

Chapters Four and Five list generic activities for using video as a catalyst for thinking. The activities in Chapter Four are designed for children in kindergarten through third grade; those in Chapter Five are suitable for children in fourth through sixth grades. Within each chapter the activities are divided according to subject and/or type of activity—for example, using video to understand the elements of a story. Chapter Six provides examples of how to link activities with specific video titles. The activities are divided by subject and age group. Regardless of the age group of your students, you will probably want to browse through all three of these chapters. You may spot activities designed for a different age group that you could adapt to fit your own classroom.

Finally, Chapter Seven offers educators suggestions for helping parents to cope with the onslaught of home videos and to use videos for learning at home.

Three supplemental sections are also included.

The first section lists more than 500 video titles, along with producer/distributor information and appropriate age groups. With very few exceptions, the list contains titles licensed for home use. To aid educators in making choices appropriate to specific classroom subjects, the videos listed are described using 17 broad categories: Adaptation, Animals, Animation, Biography, Coming of Age, Environment, Fairy Tales & Legends, Family, Fantasy (8 & Up), Fine Arts, History, Language Arts, Multiculture, Music, Reference, Science, and Travel. Also included are series of videos from CC Studios (Children's Circle), From the Brothers Grimm, Rabbit Ears Productions, Reading Rainbow, Stories To Remember, and WonderWorks.

The second section lists organizations concerned with children's video and distributors of children's video.

The third section is an annotated bibliography of print resources, including books about literature, books about media, books about child development and children, and additional useful books of a general nature.

The supplemental material is followed by a glossary of useful terms, including the much-debated "Public Performance Rights."

Acknowledgments

Beyond TV: Activities for Using Video with Children began as a 32-page handbook called *Encourage Media Literacy! 161 Activities Too Good To Miss for Ages 5–11*, which I wrote in 1986 with Constance Turner, director of the Western Suffolk Teacher's Center in New York. Grateful acknowledgment is made to Constance Turner for her role as coauthor of the handbook, and to Tim Ditlow, president of Listening Library in Old Greenwich, Connecticut, who gave me, as editor of *Children's Video Report*, a grant to write the handbook.

In addition, I owe special thanks to teachers Patricia Dresden, Elizabeth Fee, Leita Hamill, Jane Phend, Sonja Robinson, Eileen Simon, Brian Walsh, and Sigourney Wright, who is also the mother of four eager videophiles. They have all provided countless ideas and opportunities for putting the activities generated by this book into practice.

Thanks also go to Ron Slaby and Ellen Wartella, who research children's reactions to media, to Jean Lawler, former teacher and present-day computer and video expert, and to Janet Eckert from the Western Massachusetts Regional Library System.

Heartfelt appreciation goes also to Jack Bierman, Tom Cox, Jane Cross, Jane Hadley, Genevieve Kazdin, Myer Kutz, Mary Ann Pierce, Stanley Stillman, John Weber, and Nancy Wright for helping me to refine my thinking about children and video.

My thanks as well to Karen Hilton, mother of three and a current student of library sciences, and to Lucy Borge, Susan

Scher, Bonnie Watkins, Patricia Williams, and Carolyn Wright, mothers who care about what their children watch and who have become personally involved in affecting what all children see.

Finally, thanks to Heather Cameron and Beth Blenz-Clucas from ABC-CLIO, who saw larger horizons for the small maroon handbook and invited me to venture forth.

Introduction

As a medium, video is a double-edged sword. On one side, its message has the potential to touch children deeply. It can act as a catalyst for thinking, inspiring them to learn. Video can show children worlds they might not otherwise enter. But it also has the potential to anesthetize its audience and can turn an alert, active child into a cranky, belligerent, and seemingly unintelligent creature who stares into space and is barely capable of responding to or interacting with other human beings. The reasons for this "vidiot" syndrome are not wholly understood, but anyone who has witnessed it cannot help but be concerned about its effects.

Children today choose to spend a great deal of their time with television, video games, and computers—their electronic friends. Are these young people missing the adventures and the daydreams endemic to childhood? If so, how is this loss going to affect them? They are growing up in a sophisticated and technologically advanced era, in a world quite different from that of 50 or even 30 years ago. Yet, along with this technological progress, which affects all aspects of modern life, the question arises: are children learning the necessary skills to function successfully in this media-filled society? Are they being taught how to judge appropriately what they see, in order to be able to discern the truth? Along with their ability to use computers, VCRs, and video games, are their thinking skills being challenged and nurtured appropriately, in a way that will lead them to become lovers of the spoken and written word, solvers of problems, and contributors to society?

Media literacy is the acquisition of critical viewing skills that enable an individual to understand and use newspapers, radio, television, computers, film, and video. It is becoming increasingly important for teachers and librarians to assist children in developing the necessary skills to be discriminating media consumers. Video can be entertaining, and it is generally high on most children's lists of favorite ways to spend time. In order not to be seduced by video or become addicted to it, children need to know its dangers as well as its assets.

Children clearly benefit from media literacy programs that stress the acquisition of critical viewing skills through well-defined discussions and related activities. Further, such sessions provide them with opportunities both to listen to their peers' points of view and to offer their own opinions and concerns. With proper guidance, students do listen to other children's interpretations of and reactions to video programs. The group experience encourages students to listen and thus develop an essential tool for better communication.

Such processes are essential if students are to develop higher levels of inquiry, logic, and reasoning, which in turn will lead to more discriminating viewing. Only when students understand the material and can explain or summarize it in a discussion are they ready to analyze and synthesize the literary elements that may be portrayed through complex sound and video images. It is only then that they are able to begin evaluating a program's value. In addition to comprehending the literary elements of video, it is crucial for children to understand basic video production techniques. By manipulating the medium, students better understand how video is created. This gives them additional tools for evaluating the videos they view both inside and outside the classroom. Because television has been considered a wasteland by many, video has engendered low expectations as an educational tool. However, when used thoughtfully and in moderation, in conjunction with well-planned activities, video can stimulate, clarify, and move. It can spark new interests and motivate children to think about new topics, concepts, and ideas.

Quality video programming, thoughtfully integrated into the curriculum, provides young people with an intense and provocative experience that clearly affects their thoughts and feelings. Children, as well as adults, gain perspective and understanding when experiencing a video in conjunction with discussions and activities. Educators know the impact that a well-organized and clearly designed media program can have on students. For this reason, *Beyond TV* brings together ideas, suggestions, and activities for using video as a catalyst for thinking—to enhance and enrich classroom education and promote media literacy among today's children—and tomorrow's leaders.

Beyond TV
ACTIVITIES FOR USING VIDEO WITH CHILDREN

ONE

Guidelines for Building a Video Collection

The videocassette recorder exerted a powerful influence on the 1980s, and statistics show that VCRs are now almost everywhere that children are. In the United States, 95 percent of elementary and secondary schools own at least one VCR. Only ten years after their introduction, reasonably priced videos are now in more than two-thirds of all public libraries. The *New York Times* reported in August 1989 that while 55 to 60 percent of families without children have VCRs, 75 to 80 percent of families with children do. In 1981, there were 5,500 video specialty stores in the country; there are now more than 29,000. The influx of video into children's lives is certainly significant.

A VCR, however, is only as powerful as the tape that goes into it. Good programming can bring the whole world into a classroom, auditorium, or living room. It can enhance basic skill development so that learning can take place, and it has the potential to motivate. If used properly, video is, in fact, a resource for learning. But how does an audiovisual librarian decide which children's videos to purchase? How do teachers select videos to show in their classrooms? What do you do if you are just beginning to think about purchasing tapes for a school or library?

In both school systems and public libraries, AV librarians serve an educational function. Both types of institutions have similar goals—to offer the best children's programming available, whether it is to be used as an instructional tool to enhance an existing curriculum or in the home to educate or entertain. The actual tapes selected by the two media experts may be different, but their goals are the same.

Video in the Classroom

Video has become an integral part of the instructional program. It is another mode of instruction that allows teachers to provide the core curriculum for all students. Teachers want programming that fits into their curriculum and that can be viewed during a class period while leaving time for discussion. They welcome guides and supplementary materials with ideas for pre- and postviewing discussions as well as additional information that increases the value of the programming.

Although children may enjoy the novelty of a video game, they learn best from well-planned lessons offering repetition and reinforcement. So a student who is having difficulty reading *Charlotte's Web* can watch a tape of the movie based on the book and participate in a discussion in order to appreciate the genius of E. B. White's creation. Students who have read and enjoyed the book also benefit from such a review.

Video and the Public Library

Public librarians, on the other hand, are looking for quality children's programs of a general nature. An increasing number of patrons are visiting the children's rooms in their public libraries in search of tapes to check out for their children. Many libraries budget for tapes with public performance rights for public screenings (see Appendix B) as well as for videos that can be lent or rented to patrons and community groups. Thus librarians are seeking to purchase tapes that are both educational and entertaining.

Frank Woods, AV consultant for the Vermont Department of Libraries in Montpelier, said in a telephone interview that "the overriding consideration is quality—the story line, the technical quality, does it hold up as a film?" He went on to say, "We want video to broaden our patron's experiences, so we don't cater to rural isolation. Thus, we own *Teach Me To Dance* (Films, Inc.), about a Ukrainian girl experiencing discrimination in a small Canadian town, as well as *Goggles* (Coronet/MTI), about inner-city life, Disney's *Anne of Green Gables*, and even some public domain cartoon classics."

Libraries with existing 16mm collections already have a proclivity toward educational product. They are now purchasing educational titles in video format as well as videos produced for the home market. These include adaptations of children's literature (*The Electric Grandmother*, LCA), sing-along performance tapes (*Raffi in Concert with the Rise and Shine Band*, A&M), activity tapes (*Jim Henson Play-Along Video* series, Warner), and other entertaining live-action and animated productions. Libraries do not, however, want guidebooks or game parts, since such items are easily lost, thus diminishing the tape's value to patrons.

Conceptualizing the Children's Collection

Before beginning to research video distributors and specific titles to purchase, both teachers and librarians need to define their collections' purposes and create guidelines for selecting tapes. The AV librarian's ultimate goal is to build an exemplary collection. Teachers want collections that will enhance their schools' curricula, and public librarians want to strengthen the children's holdings in their libraries. In each case, the goal of the collection will probably be to meet the needs of a variety of children by providing a wide assortment of quality tapes.

Even before beginning to select tapes, librarians must settle questions on how the collection will be handled. These include questions on such issues as the following:

Money. Where is the money going to come from to pay for the tapes? Will it come from the library's regular acquisitions fund, or from another source or sources?

Space. Where will the tapes be kept? In a school, tapes can be kept in a media room or in the school library. In a public library, children's tapes could be kept with the rest of the library's video collection. A better alternative, however, is to keep them in the children's room, where a children's librarian is available to provide assistance and suggestions to both young patrons and their parents. The ideal arrangement would be to have videos shelved with the books—so that, for example, the book *Corduroy* is shelved next to the CC Studios tape *Corduroy and Other Bear Stories.*

Access. Who will have access to the tapes? Are they kept behind the checkout desk or in a locked cabinet, or are they accessible to patrons? How old must a child be to check out tapes? Will children with library cards have free access to the complete holdings of the library? The American Library Association (ALA) has published a report on this subject titled "Access for Children and Young People to Videotapes and Other Nonprint Formats." Copies are available on request from the ALA (see Appendix B for the address). The reader may also want to request a copy of the "Freedom To View" statement endorsed by ALA on June 28, 1979.

Age guidelines. What will be the librarian's responsibility in terms of providing age guidelines? With most books this issue does not arise; when children hear or read stories, they create images in their minds that are manageable for them—images that are neither too frightening nor too threatening. When children see images, however, whether in picture books or videos, those images are there to be seen regardless of their appropriateness, and they have a greater chance of remaining with children. (See Chapters Three and Seven for more information on age guidelines.)

Evaluating and Selecting Videos

When evaluating children's programming, it is critical not to lose sight of the fact that the tapes are for children. Depending on their age and experience, children react differently to visual images. Thus, when reviewers for the newsletter *Children's Video Report* evaluate a tape, they carefully scrutinize the story's appropriateness for its intended audience. This is especially critical in considering programming for very young children. (See Chapter Three for guidelines on age appropriateness.) Other critical factors are the quality of the tape's production and its overall appeal to its intended audience. Most children's programming falls somewhere between mind-numbing garbage and timeless classic. Such in-between fare is fine for video stores, but it does not belong in school or library collections, which should contain only the best tapes available.

California has developed a recommended literature list for kindergarten through grade 12. From that list a supplementary list of films and videos has been compiled that fits into specific curriculum areas throughout the grades. Such a list provides a good starting point for building a collection. (See Appendix B for information on how to obtain this list.)

School librarians just beginning to build collections will want to select tapes that teachers support, including ones they are already using in their curriculum. A public library might begin by choosing titles that are adaptations of Caldecott winners, such as "Make Way for Ducklings" (Weston Woods), which is included on the CC Studios tape *Smile for Auntie and Other Stories,* or the tape *Noah's Ark* (Hi-Tops), with James Earl Jones narrating. Both school and library collections would benefit from titles such as *Molly's Pilgrim* (Phoenix) and *Walking on Air* (Public Media Video). In each of these, viewers will encounter ways of life they probably will never experience. Each video also features well-developed characters and a story with universal appeal.

Whenever possible, a librarian should read at least one critical review of a tape before purchasing it. If possible, the

8 Guidelines for Building a Video Collection

tape should also be previewed before it is purchased. Too often librarians select tapes from catalogues without prior knowledge of their quality or content. A better idea is to organize a previewing committee or committees. For teachers these might be organized by subject matter, grade, location, district, or county. Librarians might organize committees by fiction and nonfiction. General questions to ask when considering or previewing a tape include the following:

- ❑ To whom is the tape targeted? Will it appeal to the targeted audience? Who else might gain from seeing it?
- ❑ Where else can the same information be found? Is video the best medium for communicating the idea?
- ❑ Is the plot understandable, interesting, and challenging? Is conflict dealt with appropriately for the tape's intended audience?
- ❑ Are the tape's instructional goals clearly met? Is the information delivered in an interesting manner, with respect for the intended audience? Is the information accessible to the intended audience?
- ❑ What values does the tape reinforce?

For more information on what to consider when previewing a tape, see Chapter Two.

A number of publications now either include or specialize in video reviews. These include *Booklist, Library Journal, Publishers Weekly, School Library Journal, Video Librarian* (P.O. Box 2725, Bremerton, WA 98310; phone 206-377-2231), *Video Rating Guide for Libraries* (phone 800-422-2546), and, of course, *Children's Video Report* (P.O. Box 3228, Princeton, NJ, 08543-3228; phone 609-452-7980). Several parenting magazines and newspapers also feature regular video columns.

Those interested in video collections for children should attend film and video festivals whenever possible to preview new programming and meet people with similar interests:

- ❑ The American Film and Video Association (920 Barnsdale Road, Suite 152, La Grange, IL 60525;

phone 708-482-4000) holds an annual festival for nontheatrical film and video. Programming includes all types of instructional media for the classroom as well as home video. Media professionals in schools and public libraries will find this gathering most useful.
- ❏ The Birmingham International Educational Film Festival (P.O. Box 2641, Birmingham, AL 35291-0665; phone 205-250-2711) provides exposure for independent, commercial, and student film and video producers. The organizers' goal is to identify films and videotapes that prove educational media can be simultaneously educational and entertaining. Currently, 17 categories of films are represented, including several that are targeted to children in kindergarten through sixth grade.
- ❏ The Chicago International Festival of Children's Films, sponsored by Facets Video (phone 800-331-6197), holds screenings of live-action and animated shorts and feature films. Children are encouraged to attend.
- ❏ The National Educational Film & Video Festival (314 East Tenth Street, Room 205, Oakland, CA 94606; phone 415-465-6885) is a competitive festival for educational and nontheatrical and special interest productions intended for use in schools, universities, TV broadcast, libraries, museums, instructional TV, and the home market. The festival published *Curriculum Guide: Using Film and Video To Teach Writing and Critical Thinking,* which was cowritten with the Oakland Unified School District and includes chapters on using video with literature, across the curriculum, and in English as a second language classes.
- ❏ The National Film & Video Market (P.O. Box 11274, Memphis, TN 38111; phone 901-763-5566) is a four-day trade show designed for buyers of media, where distributors meet with people who buy product. Companies show product according to

10 Guidelines for Building a Video Collection

both schedules and individual requests. Substantial discounts are available to people who buy during the show.

Between school and home, children watch a great deal of video. Those in decision-making roles have a responsibility to use the utmost care in selecting programming that celebrates the media with both challenging content and images that are appropriate for their intended audience.

From *I'd Like To Teach the World To Sing* (KidSongs series), produced by View-Master. Photo courtesy of Warner Bros. Records, Inc.

TWO

Using Video as a Catalyst for Thinking

Properly used, video can serve as a way to challenge, motivate, and inspire children to think and explore new ideas and ways of looking at the world. This chapter explains how to select videos that will serve as a catalyst for thinking, and then explains what to do both before and after showing a video in order to facilitate thought and discussion among students.

Selecting Videos for Classroom Use

Use the following questions as guidelines for evaluating the appropriateness of a particular video as an instructional tool:

- Is video the best medium for communicating this specific information, or would a book or teacher do it better?
- Does the content of the tape extend the curriculum?
- Is the video appropriate for the age of the audience? At the same time, will it cause them to stretch in any way?
- Is the message important for the students to hear, see, and feel?
- How long is the video? Is this an appropriate length for the students, or would they do better seeing

similar content but in a shorter or longer format?
- How much time will be needed to prepare the class for viewing this video?
- Does the video make interesting use of language, visuals, textures, shapes, sounds?
- If appropriate, are a variety of ethnic groups represented in the video?
- Does the video show children something they might not otherwise see?
- Is the video timely and in good condition, with a clear sound track?

Facilitating Children's Responses to Video

The VCR is reserved, the tape is ordered, and you feel confident it will enhance the curriculum. Now what? How do you introduce the tape to the class? What do you tell them about it before they see it? How much questioning and clarifying do you do before pushing the "play" button? These are items to consider before showing the video to a class:

- In order to draw from your students and to learn what information they are bringing to the video, brainstorm for prior knowledge about the story or content matter before showing the tape.
- If the group is not reading yet, tell them the title. Also, for many children a short description of the video will help them approach the tape's content. You may decide that it is more effective just to give the title.
- Notify viewers ahead of time if the video is in black and white or if it does not have any dialogue. As long as children know what to expect beforehand, they tend to accept such tapes; if they are not told, they sometimes feel cheated.
- When you start the video, place the VCR counter on 0000. Suggest to older students that if something occurs in the story that may be useful to discuss,

they should jot down the counter number. This will enable them to go to the VCR, fast forward the video, and retrieve the segment to be discussed with their classmates.
- Stopping the tape during viewing is recommended only occasionally. It can be an effective way to encourage children to make predictions about a character or outcome of the story, but it does interfere with the story's rhythm. Do it, but only very selectively.
- Whenever possible, videotape discussions and activities to show children their responses. This is also useful for highlighting students' growth over time.

After the Video: Facilitating Discussion

Perhaps the most challenging part of teaching with video is getting a discussion going after the viewing. Each child is unique; each learns and responds to the world differently. Some are extroverts who reply to questions spontaneously, seemingly without taking time to think about their answers. Others need time for reflection, or may be reluctant to offer opinions even with prodding and support. Most students probably fall somewhere in the middle. They try to participate, since that is what's expected of them, but they are not at all sure that doing so is in their own best interest. One of your goals as an educator is to set a tone that encourages and supports students' input, so they are willing to take risks, raise their hands, and actively participate in the discussion.

As the leader, you set the tone for the discussion. Is the purpose of a question to find the "right" answer or to offer students a forum for exploration of ideas? This is as important for teachers of preschoolers as it is for those working with postdoctoral candidates. Ask questions that go beyond "Did you like it?" and that elicit responses beyond reciting facts pertaining to the tape's content. Divergent questioning (no one right answer) encourages and challenges children to think hard in order to explore many facets of the material. Let students know you respect thinking and the exploration of ideas. At the same time, become involved in the discussion. Offer your opinions. By showing your interest and caring about students' thoughts, you encourage their participation.

Questioning is only one technique to help children explore and learn from watching a video. Another way to stimulate further thought and discussion is to present your own thoughts or opinions on a matter in a declarative statement. To reaffirm a student's response, summarize what you understand to have been said. This gives students more time to think, which may result in additional comments. Or, if you are not clear about a student's reply, say so and ask the child to explain further. Research indicates, however, that responding to a question with another one probably is not useful. It may discourage additional questions. Are your students more involved and do they respond with greater depth when you pose questions or when you engage them with a declarative statement? Test this and decide for yourself.

Encourage children to ask each other questions when something is not clear to them. By inviting a child to elaborate on a point you may help him or her to explore an issue further. Research also suggests that when students respond to other students' questions, they give longer and more complex answers than when responding to a teacher's question. Children often like to make their own discoveries or hear the "ahas" from other children rather than from adults.

The following ideas can help to start a discussion and keep it going:

- In *Taking Advantage of the Media* (Routledge & Kegan Paul, 1986), Laurene K. Brown offers three suggestions for discussion starters with young children: "What if . . . ?" "Why do you suppose . . . ?" "Let's pretend . . . ." At the end of a discussion, ask children, "How did you feel when . . . and what do you think now?"
- Richard Lacey suggests in his book *Seeing with Feeling: Films in the Classroom* (W. B. Saunders, 1972) using what he calls an "image-sound skim." This is

After the Video: Facilitating Discussion 15

an effective technique to discover children's thoughts about video programs. Immediately following a viewing, go around the room asking students to state an image or sound that comes to mind when thinking of the video they have just seen. Make note of recurrent themes and explore them further with the class.

- Encourage children to speak in complete sentences when talking about videos. Ask them to give reasons for their answers and to back up their reasons with pertinent information from the video. If any students pause in the middle of their responses, give them time to collect their thoughts and begin speaking again before helping with their response or asking the next question.
- If any students do not participate when questioned, explain that you will give them time for reflection and then come back to them a second time.
- When you think it might be useful for the class to explore something further, ask, "Is there anything more?" or "Anything else?" or make a statement out of a student's response. If the discussion comes to a standstill, ask who, what, why, where, when, and how questions to get the class engaged again.
- Another way to generate thought during the discussion is to pose questions and ask the class to respond on paper. This gives everyone an opportunity to respond, not just the few who are called on during class discussions. Ask for volunteers to share their entries.
- To wrap up after a video discussion, ask the children to write about a specific topic, solicit suggestions for topics, or offer them free choice. Because this is both a writing exercise and an opportunity for them to reflect on the video, request full sentences.
- Sometimes after watching a video, rather than talk about it, give children time to respond privately. Ask them to write or draw on paper, perhaps in a video journal, with pencils, crayons, felt-tip pens,

paint, or any format other than verbal expression. This is particularly helpful for video stories that are emotionally demanding. Invite each student to share his or her entry with a partner and then perhaps with the entire group, giving each the option to refuse.
- At the end of a discussion, ask students if there were any parts of the video that were unclear. See if others in the class can clear up unanswered questions for the puzzled students.

The Importance of "Deep" Questioning

All children benefit from thoughtful questions that engage them to think beyond the obvious. Facts that are elicited from convergent questioning (one right answer)—the undemanding "What is the name of the person who is buried in Grant's tomb?" type of questioning that is all too common in many classrooms—can be learned by reviewing the material. In their superb book, *Exploring Books with Gifted Children* (Libraries Unlimited, 1980), Nancy Polette and Marjorie Hamlin apply Bloom's classification system to asking thought-provoking questions about books. Bloom's six categories—knowledge, comprehension, application, analysis, synthesis, and evaluation—illustrate the importance of questioning deeply, not just widely.

Polette and Hamlin offer six categories to use with questioning: quantity questions, reorganization questions, supposition questions, viewpoint questions, involvement questions, and forced association questions. This system easily applies to video and to all children, not just those classified as gifted. Using the video adaptation of Charles Perrault's *Red Riding Hood* (SVS) as an example, questions might run something like this:

- Quantity questions: How many reasons can you think of for Red to want to visit her grandmother? What do you think Red saw on her walk in the woods after she strayed from the path?

The Importance of "Deep" Questioning 17

- Reorganization questions: What would the wolf have done if Red had not deviated from the path? What else could Red and Woodsman put inside the wolf so he couldn't move very fast?
- Supposition questions: Suppose the wolf were kindly, how would that change the story? Suppose Red went to Grandmother's house with a friend. What do you think might have happened?
- Viewpoint questions: How might the wolf have responded to Red if she were Big Red and carrying a large pointed stick? How would you tell the story from the wolf's point of view?
- Involvement questions: If you were Red and were asked to go through the woods alone for the first time to deliver food to your Granny, how would you feel? If your Granny had been sick in bed like Red's, what would you want to bring her in your basket?
- Forced association questions: How are Ramona Quimby and Little Red Riding Hood alike? Do you know anyone who is like the wolf or Little Red Riding Hood?

A classroom that reflects intellectual curiosity and excitement about learning is brimming with questions—teacher to student, student to teacher, and student to student—back and forth with no prescribed formula. People learn from inquiry and investigating, from honest questions, and from each other, as well as from their mistakes. The goal of a good discussion is to get everyone thinking, probing, and thinking some more. Using video as a catalyst for students' own explorations is a superb way to encourage thinking.

18 Using Video as a Catalyst for Thinking

From *Hawk, I'm Your Brother* (Stories of American Indian Culture series). Photo courtesy of Best Film & Video Corp.

THREE

Children's Media Needs by Age

Preschool

The 5-year-olds who walk through the door on the first day of kindergarten come with varying degrees of understanding about what goes on in the television to bring them "Mister Rogers' Neighborhood," "Sesame Street," and "Muppet Babies." As preschoolers, these same children were exploring everything, getting a sense of who they were and the parameters of their world. They worked to make sense of what they saw—what is real, what is pretend—and they asked a thousand questions. Because the fast pace of life often seemed confusing to them, they found familiar, evenly paced, and reassuring videos such as *Corduroy and Other Bear Stories* (CC Studios) and *Here We Go,* Volumes 1 and 2 (Just for Kids), the most meaningful.

Young children do not differentiate between real and pretend; they believe what they see on the screen. Hence, wolves in videos can hurt them just as much as wolves in their living rooms, and Mr. Rogers lives in the TV, just as a friend lives around the corner. Hedda Sharapan, from "Mister Rogers' Neighborhood," tells of the time a young child asked Mr. Rogers how he got out of the TV. In his patient and supportive way, Rogers explained to the child in simple words how television works. The boy nodded his head during the discussion, and then asked how Mr. Rogers was going to get back into the TV.

At the same time, preschoolers have not yet developed the defenses to protect themselves from what they see on the screen. Video contains strong images, often combined with dramatic music that heightens the emotional tone. Confusing and frightening images—monsters, witches, wolves, and fighting—can be overwhelming to small children. Superheroes and powerful characters who lose control and express anger with a punch are also confusing for children who are just learning to express anger in words. When they listen to stories, children create their own pictures of the action. But hearing a story about animals fighting is very different from actually seeing it happen on screen. The familiar story of *Pinocchio* is a classic example of a film that seems charming to adults but that can terrify small children. Parents who remember seeing Walt Disney's adaptation of Carlo Collodi's story when they were young are eager to share it with their children, but very young children cannot assimilate the frightening scenes about the wooden boy who experiences adventures of whale-sized proportions.

By the time children are 4 or 5 years old, they are less frightened by scary stories than they would have been at 3, but they still find it reassuring when a scary video has a happy ending. Even though they might be scared while watching it, at the end they feel a sense of accomplishment and bravery for having stuck with it. They have survived!

Kindergarten through Third Grade

Entering kindergarten is an important milestone in every child's life. Because there are many children in a class, each receives less attention from the teacher than he or she may be used to receiving. School thus forces children to become more independent, if they are not already striving toward such independence. Programming with a theme that combines independence with the desire for security is appealing to children of this age. Many of the titles in CC Studio's extensive collection feature characters (animal or otherwise) who assert a bit of independence, go off on journeys, and return home feeling ever so proud of their accomplishments. These are wonderful videos for children 5 and 6 years old.

Most 5-year-olds respond well to alphabet tapes with live-action footage. Tapes such as *Animal Alphabet* (Warner), *Animal ABCs* (Creative Video Concepts), *Richard Scarry's Best Alphabet Video Ever* (Random House), and *Richard Scarry's Best Counting Video Ever* (Random House) will challenge and engage them. And, of course, kindergartners love to sing. *I'd Like To Teach the World To Sing*, in ViewMaster's Kidsongs series, is a good choice because within the context of a story line the effervescent Kidsong Kids sing songs while wearing costumes from around the world.

Lyle, Lyle Crocodile: The Musical (Hi-Tops) is an adaptation of the popular picture book, a fantasy story with just the right amount of humor. Dr. Seuss tapes (from Random House, Playhouse, and other distributors) engage viewers with Seuss's wonderful use of language, which kindergartners enjoy because they are in on the joke, knowing which words are nonsense and which are real. These tapes are also delightfully animated. Because 5-year-olds may still be a bit shaky in terms of what is real and what is not, it is best to avoid programming with frightening images. And, because children this age are just venturing out into the world, trusting that it is a good place to go, programming that might create anxieties about injury or abandonment should be avoided.

Kindergartners and first graders also love stories about real-life children who, like themselves, are members of a family and who are experiencing school and friends and learning about the intricacies of life. *The Story About Ping and Other Stories* (CC Studios) and the *Bank Street Read-Along Story Videos* (Best Film & Video) fit this bill perfectly.

As children enter first grade, many are reading, but many are not. What both groups have in common is their love for a good story. The fact that children are not yet reading does not mean that they are not capable of following more complex story lines. Beverly Cleary's Ramona books and

22 Children's Media Needs by Age

Warner Home Video's adaptations (initially seen on PBS) are tailor-made for this age group. Ramona is a three-dimensional character with whom children (boys as well as girls) can readily identify. She gets into scrapes, thinks in black and white, and is venturing off to school, where she wants others to like her. The live-action adaptations are quick to spark the imagination and are beautifully produced.

First graders (and older children as well) who are thinking about taking ballet lessons will love *I Can Dance* (JCI), which introduces children to ballet with a blend of rigor and romance. And for those who love the fantasy world of animation and wild and crazy beasts, *The Maurice Sendak Library* (CC Studios) offers animated adaptations of *Where the Wild Things Are, In the Night Kitchen,* and *The Nutshell Kids.* The final segment on this tape is a superb live-action documentary, "Getting to Know Maurice Sendak." All children will benefit from hearing Sendak talk about his life as an illustrator and writer of children's books.

Most 6- and 7-year-olds are gaining in physical competence and developing gross motor coordination along with an interest in games, rules, and sports. Programming such as *Little League's Official How-To-Play Baseball by Video* (MasterVision), *Be a Magician* (Mid-Com), and *Get Ready, Get Set, Grow!* (Bullfrog Films) offers children a lot of challenging information to help them focus their newly developing abilities.

By second grade, many children think they are old enough to watch the more sophisticated programming that their older siblings are enjoying. They are savvy to the ways of school and are developing interests of their own, separate from their families'. As with all children, it is important to be aware of the sensitivities of children in this age group. As much as they want to appear rough and ready, many would sooner hop back into a lap for a cozy story than be with the big kids who are watching provocative stories that second graders might find confusing. Good programming for this age reveals a part of life that children might not otherwise see. It also offers the right combination of intrigue and comfort.

A good video for second graders is *Sometimes I Wonder* (Media Ventures), about two siblings who run away from home. They go to their grandmother's house (the grandmother is played winningly by Colleen Dewhurst) because the new baby is getting all the attention at home. From their point of view it seems that everything they do aggravates Mom, Dad, and the baby. This video has the added appeal of showing the birth of a colt and presents many opportunities for discussion. To feed their thirst for information and interesting things to consider, the *Macmillan Video Almanac for Kids* (VPI, Inc.) has eight separate segments covering such diverse topics as soap bubble magic, space, and kite flying.

Third graders are grounded in what is real and what is not. Although 8-year-olds know that what is on the screen is just a story, they are often interested in whether it really happened or not. They may ask, "Is this a true story? It could happen—right?" Children this age are beginning to look at how people outside their own families live. Videos such as *Molly's Pilgrim* (Phoenix), based on Barbara Cohen's book, offers a look at other families and cultures. It is a distinguished story, with universal appeal, about a young Russian immigrant. Because third-grade children are able to comprehend a story's nuances and understand points of view different from their own, *Molly's Pilgrim* offers an opportunity to celebrate differences that exist among peoples. "Ben's Dream," found on the tape *Fun in a Box 1* (Made-to-Order Productions), follows Ben's dream around the world as he visits many famous sights. Adapted from Chris Van Allsberg's book, the video features artfully rendered black-and-white illustrations and interesting perspectives. Spotting and locating places from the video on a map is a challenging postviewing activity.

Third graders love amassing facts about new hobbies, and *The Video Guide to Stamp Collecting* (Premiere) provides much information that will appeal to budding philatelists.

Good programming can challenge and broaden a child's knowledge base by being diverse and informative. A tape such as *A World Alive* (Sea Studios) is factual and the subjects are something children adore—animals and the wonder of this planet. *Monterey Bay Aquarium*, in VideoTours' Science/Nature Collection series gives an up-close-and-personal look at a specific aquarium and offers insights about the animals inhabiting this region of California.

Children in third and fourth grade can be passionate about causes, and currently the contenders for the number-one cause are the environment and endangered animal species. Good videos on the former are *The Rotten Truth* (3-2-1 Contact Extra series, Children's Television Workshop) and *Man of the Trees* (Music for Little People). The narration in many of the tapes produced by VideoTours (see Appendix A) includes information about the extinction and threatened extinction of animals in various parts of the globe.

Critical viewing skills that prove the most useful for students this age are those that help provide a rudimentary understanding of how videos and television programs are made. Good activities are those that look at how lights, cameras, makeup, costumes, and special effects are used to create a program. An appealing book that cleverly explains the TV phenomenon to children is Marc Brown and Laurene Krasny Brown's *The Bionic Bunny* (Little, Brown, 1984; see Appendix C).

Fourth through Sixth Grade

While myriad videos exist for teenagers and children under 8, fewer filmmakers address the needs of children 9 through 12. Most cartoons do not challenge this age group, and teenage feature films are often unsuitable for them because they contain explicit violence and sex. Children in the middle years are not critical viewers. Without prompting, they usually do not analyze and evaluate what they see and hear. They will accept and watch poor-quality programming, even though they are fully aware that it is not much good. They will sit in front of the television set talking about how dumb a program is, but they are unlikely to turn it off in favor of a good game of kickball.

Research shows that children in this age range like stories with clear plots, well-developed characters, logical settings, and conflict that makes sense within the overall story. They like slapstick humor, special effects, and real-life situations about children older than themselves. Nonfiction videos appeal to them because they are interested in new information and learning about other people. Videos such as *The Video Letter from Japan* (Asia Society) help them explore other cultures, and how-to tapes about sports, magic, cartoon drawing, and special effects in movies can serve specific needs for children with special interests.

Children in the 9- through 12-year-old group are identifying more than ever before with their peers and trying to figure out how they fit in. Like Luke Skywalker in *Star Wars*, they are on a search for self. Often, their concerns are ones that parents have trouble taking seriously. *Sweet 15* (Public Media Video) does a superior job of exploring the coming-of-age of a young girl who is concerned about friends, dresses, and a special party that is being organized for her. When her life suddenly changes, viewers see her as she refocuses on what's important. *Tuck Everlasting* (Vestron), based on Natalie Babbitt's book, asks serious questions about life, death, and the meaning of it all. Children are pulled in by the superb storytelling and soon find they are asking themselves the same questions.

Adapted from Scott O'Dell's Newbery-winning story, *Island of the Blue Dolphins* (MCA) is the true story of a nineteenth-century American Indian girl's self-reliance after she is stranded on an island off the coast of California. Fourth, fifth, and sixth graders will benefit from reading the book, watching the video, and then carefully comparing the strengths of each. It is not possible to bring much of the book to the film adaptation because the reader learns about the young girl's character through her musings, not through her interactions with others. However, the video should be evaluated on its own terms. This is an intellectual challenge that children of this age will enjoy, especially discussions dealing with the girl's characterization.

Fantasy stories and science fiction also appeal to preteens, who are stimulated by the problem solving that takes place in these stories as well as by the characters' creative outlook on life. Also, many splendid and readily available classics, such as *American Graffiti* (MCA), *David Copperfield* (MGM/UA), *Beauty and the Beast* (Nelson), and *The Man Who Would Be King* (CBS/Fox), are great for preadolescents.

It can be difficult to engage preadolescents in discussion because they are often self-conscious about stating opinions in front of their peers. Therefore, a supportive environment is important if discussions are to take place. Videos can act as vehicles for tapping into students' emerging facilities to feel compassion, tenderness, sadness, and benevolence, as well as their increasing abilities to express complex ideas. Offering thoughtful, well-produced programs can call on and reinforce such feelings.

Summary of Children's Media Needs by Age

When selecting videos for any age group, it is important to keep in mind a point made by Dr. Thomas Lickona in his book, *Raising Good Children* (Bantam, 1983): all children have a developmental need to trust adults. Thus, programs that undermine this basic trust are not in anyone's best interest.

To summarize, 5–8-year-olds look for and get the most from programming with videos having the following features:

- A story line with a clearly defined and straightforward plot:
    Encyclopedia Brown (Hi-Tops)
    The Ramona Series (Warner)
    Babar the Movie (Family Home Entertainment)
- More detailed fairy tales and fantasies:
    Beauty and the Beast (Hi-Tops)
    Out of Time (Family Express)
    The Nutcracker: A Fantasy on Ice (Vidmark)
    The Land of Faraway (Starmaker)
- More complicated story lines, with some conflict and a moral:
    Hawk, I'm Your Brother (Stories of American Indian Culture series, Best Film & Video)

The Adventures of Robin Hood (MGM/UA)
- Family musicals:
  Lyle, Lyle Crocodile: The Musical (Hi-Tops)
  Meet Me in St. Louis (MGM/UA)
- Inspirational stories:
  National Velvet (MGM/UA)
  The Red Shoes (Family Home Entertainment)
- Nonfiction:
  Home Alone (Hi-Tops; not to be confused with the 1990 feature film)
  Look What I Made: Paper Playthings and Gifts (Pacific Arts)
  Who's Afraid of Opera? (Kultur)
  A World Alive (Sea Studios)

For 5–8-year-olds, videos including graphic violence or depicting wrenching separation should be avoided.

Children in the 9–12-year-old group look for and get the most from videos with the following kinds of content:

- Stories about children their age or older:
  Tommy Tricker and the Stamp Traveller (Family Home Entertainment)
- Real-life circumstances in which characters are resolving situations that are pertinent to their own lives:
  Hockey Night (Family Home Entertainment)
  Jacob Have I Loved (Public Media Video)
- Stories that look at important life questions:
  The Autobiography of Miss Jane Pittman (Prism)
  The Diary of Anne Frank (CBS/Fox)
  Hiroshima Maiden (Public Media Video)
  Walking on Air (Public Media Video)
  The World of Anne Frank (Ergo Media)
- Stories with an element of fantasy:
  The Last Starfighter (MCA)
  Fahrenheit 451 (MCA)
- Information that helps bring clarity to the world:
  The Dream Is Alive (Finley-Holiday)

28   Children's Media Needs by Age

From Star Wars to Jedi: The Making of a Saga (CBS/Fox)
What's Happening to Me? (Starmaker)
You Can Choose series (Live Wire)

From the You Can Choose series. Photo courtesy of Live Wire Video Publishers.

FOUR

Video Activities for Kindergarten through Third Grade

Understanding the Story

STORY: BEGINNING, MIDDLE, AND END

- ❏ Sequencing events is an important skill for young children. After viewing a video, ask the children to describe what happened in the beginning, in the middle, and in the end.
- ❏ After seeing a fairy tale that is new to the class, ask for a volunteer to retell the story by answering (1) what happened first (beginning), (2) what happened next (middle), and (3) what happened last (end).
- ❏ Have the class draw a picture representing action that took place at the beginning of the video, in the middle, and at the end. Laminate the three pictures on cardboard and scramble them. Ask the class to put them in the correct order.
- ❏ After the class has seen a particular video once or twice, turn the audio off. Show the video again and ask a child to narrate the story.
- ❏ Locate a variety of wordless books and ask for a volunteer to "read" one to the group. How did the

reader know the story? Talk about the clues in the pictures. Show two videos without dialogue. How does the viewer know what is going on? Watch the videos again, and invite a volunteer to provide narration.

ELEMENTS OF A STORY

- Read a short picture book to the class. Identify the parts of the story: the plot has some form of conflict or problem that needs to be solved, the characters struggle with the conflict, and the setting establishes the time and place appropriate to the action. Ask for volunteers to offer examples of each in other stories.
- Discuss the parts of a story—plot, characters, setting, conflict or problem, and the story's resolution. Have the class create a diorama for a favorite video, including information representing all the parts of the video's story.
- Direct children's attention to a well-known fairy tale. Discuss the tale's five parts—the plot, characters, setting, the problem or conflict that needs to be solved, and the story's resolution. Change one facet of the story and discuss how this affects the story's outcome. For example, what if Cinderella had not lost her glass slipper, or Hansel and Gretel had come to a kindly witch's house? How would this change the story? Have a student retell a favorite tale with one main fact altered.

Plot

- From a recently seen video, talk about the story's plot, the series of events that when put together create a story. Show a short video and ask the children to describe the plot.

Character

- From a recently seen video, ask each child to select

one character to remove from the story. Then suggest they put themselves in the action instead. How would the story then proceed? Would the child do things differently from the character in the video? How? Would the outcome be the same or different?
- ❏ For children to care about the heroes and villains in a story, the characters must be believable. Discuss what makes a character believable. Talk about stories the class has read and discuss whether their writers succeeded in creating believable characters. Ask the class to think of characters in videos who are or are not believable.
- ❏ It is fun for children to imagine how two well-known characters from different videos might interact with each other. Have the students invent a story where, for example, Bunny from *The Velveteen Rabbit* meets Harold of *Harold and the Purple Crayon* fame.
- ❏ Words are used to describe many things, including people. Ask the children to list some words that describe a character they have just seen in a video.
- ❏ Before watching a video with several characters, make a list of words that describe people positively, such as *honest, athletic, smart, pretty, wise,* and *responsible.* How do people demonstrate these qualities? After seeing the video, repeat the exercise using characters in the video; compare the two lists.

Setting
- ❏ Draw a map of an area from a video. Show the places the characters go. What is the geography like? Locate water, mountains, and plains. Make a diorama of the country, city, town, or rural area shown in the video.

Conflict
- ❏ Interesting stories always have some form of conflict or problem. In three of the class's best-loved stories, identify the conflict and its resolution.

- Before showing a video program, present a problem faced by one of the characters in the story. Have the children think of possible ways to handle the conflict. After the viewing, talk about how the problem was eventually resolved and why that particular solution may have been chosen. How else could it have been resolved? What are some other resolutions that would work?

Resolution

- Predicting the outcome of events helps to involve students in a story. Before you start a video, tell the students that you will be stopping the video for a short discussion about the story's outcome. When you stop the tape, ask the class to predict the ending of the story. Restart the tape and watch until the end. Discuss with the class the actual outcome of the story.
- With the class, make a list of stories with characters who have magical powers. Have them imagine that one of the main characters in a video they have recently seen has been given magical powers. How might the outcome of the story change?
- After seeing several videos, invite students to choose one to make a diorama about. Include some of the following: title, set, characters, time of day, and any specific props. Display the diorama in a well-traveled area in the school or library.

STORIES AND VISUAL IMAGERY

- Read a nursery rhyme, the most basic of stories, out loud to the class. Read it a second time, and this time encourage the children to close their eyes as you read. Ask them to visualize the story by painting pictures in their minds. Encourage the children to think about details by asking questions: What color was the cow that you saw in your mind jumping over the moon? How much water did you

Understanding the Story

see in Jack's pail? or What kind of a day was it when Humpty Dumpty had his great fall? Ask for volunteers to describe what they "saw" and then ask all the children to draw their imaginings. After they share their pictures with the class, display them on the bulletin board.

❑ Read a nursery rhyme to the class and do an "image-sound skim" (see Glossary) to encourage the children to pay attention to the specific sights and sounds in the rhyme. Now, watch a video adaptation of the nursery rhyme. Discuss the differences between the children's visualizations of the story and the video, noting that all the representations are "right."

❑ Do the above activities using fairy tales instead of nursery rhymes.

❑ Choose a fairy tale and, this time, watch the video adaptation first, then read the story. Do an image-sound skim and compare the differences between hearing a story first and seeing it first.

COMPARING VIDEOS AND BOOKS

❑ Have each child write a letter or make a card for his or her favorite author or illustrator whose book has been adapted to video. The letters might explain why they liked the books and what they enjoyed about the video adaptations. To help motivate students to write thoughtful letters, show them *The Author's Eye* (Random House), a video interview with Roald Dahl that contains a charming segment in which the author shows letters he has received from students.

❑ When planning to show a video that is adapted from a book, have several copies of the book available for students to look at before or after the viewing. Compare and contrast the similarities and differences between the book and video.

DRAMATIZATION ACTIVITIES

- Break the class into small groups and instruct each group to act out in pantomime a fairy tale just seen on video. Ask each group to appoint a narrator.
- When children dramatize a story they know or have seen in a video, it increases their understanding of the story. Assign parts and invite the children to put on an impromptu play.
- After viewing a particularly colorful animated video, have the children act it out. Make simple paper-plate masks of characters from the video. Use yarn, buttons, feathers, and scraps of material to decorate the masks.
- Children love diminutive heroes and animals in children's literature because they readily identify with the characters. After seeing a video of a fairy tale or animal story, have a group of children act out the story. For fun and to help spur imaginations, have the children make their own simple costumes.
- Pantomime is a way for children to express how they feel about a situation. Give a student a short exercise to pantomime and have the class guess what is being acted out. Some suggestions might be reading a book or newspaper, comforting a crying baby, licking an ice cream cone, and waiting in line for the water fountain. Encourage children to think up some pantomimes on their own.
- After viewing a video about animals at the zoo or in the wild, walk children through becoming the animals that they saw in the video. Ask student volunteers to provide suggestions of animals they would like the class to dramatize.
- Young children enjoy pretending they are something they are not. Suggest they find places on the floor and then tell them that with a snap of your fingers they will all become popcorn machines, popping delicious popcorn to enjoy while watching the video. Then, as a surprise treat, pop some real popcorn in

class for all to enjoy while watching a video. Turn it into a science and social studies class and explain who first popped corn and how it came to be.

MUSIC AND MOVEMENT

- After watching a video with songs, replay some of the less familiar ones and sing along in order to learn the words.
- Children love to move, and often a video program with a strong musical element brings this out. Have the children do some favorite dances to the music from the video, such as the Mexican hat dance, a square dance, or the hokeypokey. Alternatively, invite students to form small groups and choreograph their own creations.
- Movement activities are a wonderful way for young children to express how they feel about a video. Structured movement exercises can bring a new dynamic into a video discussion. For example, children can bounce like a Ping-Pong ball, drift like a leaf falling from a tree, swing like a monkey, or stretch like a lion. You can assign a leader to suggest other enjoyable movement images.
- Another movement exercise encourages group cooperation. Break the class into small groups, then ask each group of children to build a VCR with their bodies. They will need a top for their VCR, sides, and a hole for the tape. Remind them to think of a machine. Turn the VCR on and insert a videocassette. They are now ready to show a great video!

ART ACTIVITIES

- Art-related activities provide an effective way to involve children in video discussions. Ask the children to paint on a piece of paper images and shapes they remember having seen in the video. Do the pictures tell a story?

- Explain to the class that they are going to design their own "video stickers," but before you give them their own special paper, you want them to draw a first draft, just like designers of store-bought stickers do. Once their drafts are completed, invite the children to draw their designs on sticker paper and cut them out.
- Point out the collage technique when watching a video with collage animation. Provide paper in a variety of colors and textures to create a large group collage. Suggest that the children close their eyes and recall an image from the video while working on the collage.
- Have students use transparencies to create pictures related to a video they have just watched. Have them use permanent markers (taking care not to mark clothes or furniture) and encourage them to fill up the entire 8½-by-11-inch space. Project the transparencies on overhead projectors. Be sure artists sign their works, so they see their names in lights!
- After showing a video that is rich in color and detail, have students create colored chalk drawings on black construction paper of the story's ending. Use nonaerosol hair spray to protect the drawings from smearing.
- Have students make tissue-paper collages of the first picture that comes to mind when they close their eyes and think of the video they have just watched. The tissue paper can be applied to construction paper using liquid starch. Black felt-tip pens produce a good contrast.

Character Art Activities

- Decorate hats with pictures and objects that symbolize a character from the video or perhaps a superhero. Have the children include important incidents in the character's life. Have a parade!

- Draw, paint, or create in nonhardening clay one of the following characters from videos: fantasy character, real person, animal, or monster. Label the characters and display them on a table.
- Encourage children to make a doll modeled after a special character in a video. Provide the students with cloth, sequins, paper, yarn, pipe cleaners, and buttons to make a paper-towel-roll body.
- Have students make mobiles that include a video's title and main characters, using a hanger, string, and colored paper. Encourage the children to think of something that symbolizes each character and draw the character holding it.

Understanding Video Production

VIDEO ELEMENTS
- Explain the parts of a book to the class: title, cover, title page, dedication, table of contents, story. Discuss the corresponding parts of a video: title, credits, story, closing credits. How are book credits different from video credits?
- Some videos tell their stories using live action (see Glossary), some use animation, and others use both techniques. Discuss examples of live-action videos and animated videos.

ACTING AND CHARACTERIZATION
- Ask for a volunteer to pantomime a particular episode from a video. Have the class guess what it is. Videotape the pantomime and then play it back and enjoy it with the class.
- After showing a live-action video, discuss the main characters. Did viewers believe the characters? What did the actors do to make themselves believable? Were the actors right for their parts? Why or why not?

ANIMATION

- Young children can have a filmmaking experience that they will thoroughly enjoy, without the need for cameras. Tape a roll of white 16mm leader film on a large piece of paper and place it on the floor. Assign sections of the leader to small groups and have them draw directly on it, using translucent magic markers. Point out the side of the leader that absorbs the ink. When fed into a projector, this film will appear animated. See *Doing the Media*, edited by Kit Laybourne and Pauline Cianciolo (McGraw-Hill, 1979), for useful suggestions for this project.
- Have students draw a character from an animated video. Suggest that they draw a thought bubble with the character's "comments" about how it feels to be famous.
- Children enjoy making their own flip books. Small white scratch pads from the five-and-ten work well for these because the paper is thin. Show the class a basic flip book (these can be purchased at many stationery or specialty stores for a couple of dollars, or you can make your own to use for demonstration). Discuss how the effect of movement was created. Have the children plan the movements they want in their flip books, such as a flower blooming, a child waving, or a person jumping. After they have planned what to draw, the students can begin their books. Using felt-tip pens, the students draw on the last page of the pad, then lay the next-to-last page over it and redraw the picture, changing it slightly in the direction of the desired movement; they continue in this manner until the movement being pictured is complete. Then, by turning to the last page of the book and flipping the pages as they go toward the front, the students can see their own animation.

COSTUMES AND SCENERY

- After showing a live-action video, discuss the clothing (costumes) of some of the characters. Why were the characters wearing their specific clothing? What else would have been appropriate?
- Sets are designed according to specific instructions given by the production team. Discuss the type of information a set conveys about a story. Have students make a diorama showing a room set or a scene that has been shot outdoors.

PRODUCING

- The producer (see Glossary) is responsible for the entire video production. Ask the children what kinds of things they think the producer does.
- Have each student identify a video he or she really liked. Discuss the production values (see Glossary) in a simple way, making note of the following: scenery, costumes, presentation of the story, and quality of the writing (the script).
- What can you learn about a producer by examining the videos he or she has produced? Look at the work of Morton Schindel (Weston Woods/CC Studios) or Joshua Greene (Stories To Remember series, *Beauty and the Beast*; *Noah's Ark*; *What's a Good Story? Beauty and the Beast*).
- As a class or individually, have students write a letter to a producer, in care of the video distributor, asking specific questions about being a producer. What does a producer do? What was it about producing that was appealing or interesting? What does he or she like about producing? What is difficult about producing? Did he or she have to take special courses to become a producer? Are there any special skills or tricks of the trade needed to become a producer?

- View videos of the same story produced by different people, such as *Beauty and the Beast*, *The Velveteen Rabbit*, or *The Elephant's Child*. Discuss the similarities and differences in the versions and the effects of different production decisions on each.
- What is scary? Discuss frightening scenes in videos. What was scary about it? Did the filmmaker intend for viewers to be scared? How did the filmmaker create a scary feeling? How did the filmmaker accomplish the frightening effect? Were special effects used?

SCRIPTING AND STORYBOARDING

- Youngsters love reading plays. Point out that productions on television and video begin with scripts. Locate plays that have been written for children to read, and during a reading group allow students to decide on parts and read through some scripts. Propose that they write their own.
- Explain to the class that when people produce a video they make a storyboard (see Glossary). The storyboard puts together the different scenes from the story. Fold a large piece of paper in four parts and draw a story with a series of events. Ask student volunteers to create a storyboard from the story.
- Ask students to think about the different activities they do in the morning before eating breakfast, such as getting out of bed, feeding the dog, or brushing their teeth. Give each child three pieces of paper or three 5-by-8-inch index cards and ask them to draw on each card a simple picture illustrating an event that occurred before breakfast. Explain that storyboards are used in the same way by filmmakers to organize a video's story. Have each student share his or her storyboard with another member of the class.

Understanding Video Production

- Provide children with cards or paper on which to create storyboards for a favorite video adventure. When the storyboards are completed, have each child exchange his or her cards with a classmate. Each child then shuffles the cards and puts them in an order that tells a story.

USING A VIDEO CAMERA

- Ask the class if any of them have seen or used a video camera (camcorder). What is it used for? Explain that the use of lights is often necessary when taping, even when shooting outside on a sunny day.
- At the beginning of the year, if your school or library has access to a video camera, tape the children introducing themselves and naming videos they like. Then show the tape to the children. Play it again at the end of the year so the children can see how they have grown.
- Children often love creating worksheets for their classmates. Tell them that after seeing a video they are going to create fun-filled worksheets about how the camera was positioned for specific shots in the video. Duplicate the worksheets and encourage the children to complete them and return them to the persons who created them, with their comments.

SOUND

- While watching a video, children are aware of the visual aspect, but often miss the role of audio/sound. Before watching a video with your students, stress the importance of sound in telling a story. Show the video a second time without the sound. Have the students take turns narrating the story.

- Discuss with students the role that sound, including music, plays in a video. How does it affect the way people respond to the program? Would the production be different without sound? Does sound ever prepare the viewer for what is about to happen?
- While watching a particularly scary video, point out the sound that accompanies the scary parts. Then play the video a second time but turn off the tape's sound and play happy music instead. Discuss the differences.
- Watch a video with the sound off. Suggest to the students that they talk about the video with a partner while watching it. Tape-record their comments and play back the recording after the viewing.

SPECIAL EFFECTS

- Some videos use many different special effects (see Glossary) to communicate a story. What popular videos have brought special effects to a new level of excellence?
- The children's book *The Bionic Bunny,* by Marc Brown and Laurene K. Brown (Little, Brown, 1984), cleverly points out the part that special effects play in creating superheroes. Read the book out loud to learn the behind-the-scenes techniques used to send Bionic Bunny leaping into TV's fantasyland. Would *The Bionic Bunny* make a good video? Discuss how a producer might go about turning the print bunny into an on-screen star.
- To make a scene scary, filmmakers create illusions with special effects. Ask students to think about shows they have seen with special effects. If there is a TV station close by, check into the possibility of taking your class there to see a special effects demonstration.

Using Video To Build Skills and Knowledge

LISTENING SKILLS

- Encourage the children to think about the word *listen*. What does it mean? Why do people listen? What do people need to do when they want to listen? Is it ever hard to listen? Are there times when listening is easy? Did they ever learn "how" to listen? What is a "good listener"? Do people ever practice listening?
- After talking about the importance of being a good listener and what one does in order to listen, divide the class into groups of two. Invite one child in each pair to tell the other a fairy tale. Then encourage the second child in the pair to tell a different fairy tale. What was fun about telling each other a story? What was difficult? What did the other person do well? What would the storyteller do differently the next time?
- The game of "telephone" promotes good listening. Sit the class in a circle and whisper a word into the ear of the child who is sitting next to you. That child whispers the word into the ear of the next child, and so on. The last child to hear the word says it aloud for everyone to hear. Encourage all children to pronounce the word carefully, even those who are missing a tooth or two!
- After seeing a video and doing an image-sound skim, choose one of the words that was given and use it for the game of telephone.
- Encouraging your class to be good listeners will in turn strengthen the children's vocabularies. Talk about words they hear in videos—big words, little words, funny words, and interesting-sounding words. Good listening is a skill that needs continual

refinement throughout the day, not just when discussing tapes. Keep track of new and/or interesting words and encourage the children to use these new words. If you compliment students as they use words in conversation, pretty soon they will begin complimenting one another.

MEDIA AWARENESS

- Why do people watch video programs? What do they learn? Poll the students to find out their favorite television or video programs and specific aspects they like about those shows.
- Children love to participate in surveys. After a full discussion of a video, have students rate it: (1) excellent, (2) very good, (3) good, (4) fair, or (5) poor. After the survey, have the children explain how they arrived at their ratings by discussing the video's story, the quality of the production, and the overall appeal of the video.
- Keep track of the videos seen by your students, along with the books that they have read. Take a tree branch and secure it in a large coffee can to simulate a small tree. After each viewing, have a child draw a picture, write the video's name with a short description, and place it on the tree.
- Ask children to list the television shows and videos they have seen in the past week. Encourage them to look for patterns in their viewing habits. Is their viewing menu balanced, with nonfiction and fiction programs, animated and live-action shows? How much TV and video are they watching each day? What other activities do they enjoy? What do they do while they are watching TV or video? How much do they remember about a program watched last week? What did they learn from it? Was it a good way to spend time? Why or why not? Query the class as to other questions they might ask about a TV show.

- Have the children write a group review of a video. Suggest that the review include information regarding the story, including the plot (series of events), setting (time in history, time of year, time of day, and where the story takes place), theme (the meaning the story has in our lives—has it changed the way we look at things?), and production, including the quality of the costumes, makeup, special effects, and the acting or animation. If your school or library has a newspaper, the editors might be interested in publishing the video review.
- Keep a log of drawings and reviews of tapes seen in class.
- Have children bring videos for "Show and Tell." The purpose of this activity is to practice critical viewing skills. The children select, with the help of their families, videos from home that they think are worthwhile and want to share with the class. Suggest that the tapes be fiction, so that each child can tell the class about his or her story's beginning and middle, but not the ending. Then, with the help of their parents, have the children select segments from their videos up to three minutes long to show the class. Send a letter to parents explaining the purpose of the activity and the parents' role. The letter might include the following suggestions:
    1. Choose with your child a tape that is worthwhile and that the class will benefit from knowing about. (The tapes chosen by the children will improve as the year goes on and they become more discriminating viewers.)
    2. Help your child plan what to say to the class about the tape's beginning and middle.
    3. Help your child select one short segment, time it, and, if allowed by the school, run the VCR.

After showing the segment, the child calls on other children in the class and answers their questions about the video. Children in the audience are not to talk about whether or not they have seen the tape; they should only ask questions. This is difficult for children, but it is excellent practice in good listening.

STORYTELLING

- Discuss storytelling with the children. Ask them such questions as the following: Where do stories come from? Have they ever made up stories? Do they know anyone who likes to tell stories? What kinds of stories do they like to listen to? Who is their favorite storyteller? Why? What is it about that person's storytelling style that encourages a listener to pay attention?
- Every video tells a story, whether it is a "once upon a time" video or one demonstrating how to play baseball. Discuss the elements that make someone a good storyteller, such as knowledge of the story, an expressive voice, and contact with the audience. All of these characteristics make the story come alive. Do the children know any local storytellers? Invite a local storyteller to class to share a story.

SCIENCE AND SOCIAL STUDIES

- After screening a video title about space exploration, display a model of a spaceship or space station. Talk to the class about what they think life will be like in the year 2020. Encourage them to let their imaginations go wild!
- Research an idea or place that was talked about in a video, such as an island, something about clouds, an unusual word or term, an animal, an occupation, a country or foreign language, or a food that looks interesting.
- In order to introduce a sense of geography, place a map of the world on a bulletin board. Whenever you show a video that mentions a foreign place, have a student place a pin on the map with the video's name and the newly learned location.

Using Video To Build Skills and Knowledge 47

- Draw a time line (you may want to mark it with decades rather than individual years) and post it on a bulletin board. When you know the year that a video story took place, write the title on the time line.
- To put a particular video in historical context, use a large piece of colored yarn to show when the story takes place relative to the present. Use a scale in which one inch equals ten years.
- Discuss and list on the chalkboard all the real and imaginary places that the children have visited in videos. One of the beauties of video is that it can take us places we might not otherwise go. What does this mean? For what videos is it true? Does it mean just traveling, or does it go beyond places to cultures, experiences, points of view? Discuss this in light of a video the class has recently seen.

THINKING SKILLS

- This activity encourages comparison. List with the students all the videos they can remember that include stepmothers, or animals with major parts, or creatures that speak, or wonderful magical events that could not really happen. See what comparisons can be made in each category.
- Discuss stereotypes, particularly those seen on TV or in videos. What happens when people think in stereotypical terms? Why does this happen? What characters come to mind who are stereotypes?
- During video discussions in the fall, list or tape-record students' comments. Ask questions about the characters in the video—are they interesting? Believable? Realistic? Which characters are interesting? Believable? Realistic? Why? Continue taping discussions throughout the year so that growth in the quality of the discussions can be observed.
- It is important to encourage children to think about what they have seen and to talk about the theme

of the story as well as the parts they liked and did not like. Ask them if they think viewing the tape was a worthwhile way to spend time and whether or not they would recommend it to a friend.

Using Puppets to Build Thinking Skills

- Children are easily engaged by hand puppets. By using a puppet to ask shy children questions about a video, a teacher or librarian can encourage them to participate in discussions.
- Young children love puppets. Make a basic paper-bag puppet of a character from a video. Give the puppet a childlike personality and talk through with it how to solve a problem. Perhaps the puppet is Goldilocks and she is wondering if she should return to the three bears' house to apologize for having wreaked havoc there. Ask her why she would go back and why she would not. Ask students for their ideas as to whether she should return to the bears' house.
- Have the children make their own paper-bag puppets of a funny character from a video. Encourage the students to pretend to be the character as he or she tries to solve a problem. Discuss different strategies for problem solving.

Understanding Real versus Pretend

- For younger children who still may not be able to distinguish between what is real and what is pretend, invite each child in the class to make a paper-bag mask of a favorite imaginary character seen in a video. Encourage them to pretend to be the character.
- After watching a fanciful video, ask the class if the events in the story could really happen. Discuss the differences between real and pretend. Ask the class to name some videos that include action that could not really happen.

Exploring Feelings

- Before watching a particularly poignant video, ask the children to think about all of the different feelings that exist. List them on the chalkboard. After seeing the video, have them divide a piece of paper into four equal parts and draw four different feelings that the video evoked. As the students draw, note their conversation with each other for later discussion.
- Before showing a video that deals with emotional issues, select a short segment that evokes feelings. Show the entire video, then give each child a piece of paper and ask them to fold their papers in half. Now fast forward to the segment you selected earlier and show it again. Ask the children to draw a picture about the feelings the segment evoked in them. After they have completed their pictures, ask them to think about an experience in their own lives that evoked a similar feeling and to draw this. If children have difficulty selecting from their own lives, suggest they think about someone they know. Asking for volunteers to share their experiences and pictures may help others to remember their own.

And Just for Fun

- Stop! Don't throw out that old 16mm film projector. Children love using their hands to create shadows with light, and the projector is perfect for illuminating their creations. Use it without film and have the children create shadow characters and stories. Locate books showing how to create wonderful shadows using hands and arms.

50 Video Activities: Kindergarten through Third Grade

From *Starlight Hotel*. Photo courtesy of Republic Pictures Home Video.

FIVE

Video Activities for Fourth through Sixth Grade

Understanding the Story

ELEMENTS OF A STORY

- ❏ Discuss the elements of a story—plot, characters, setting, conflict or problem, and the resolution or climax of the story (the most exciting part). Good stories also have particular themes and moods. Have individuals or groups create dioramas depicting a favorite video, and try to include information representing all the elements of the video's story. Is it possible to re-create a feeling or a mood?
- ❏ With the class, analyze a video in terms of its story. Is the video true to life? Does it matter if it is not realistic? Are there parts of the story that do not make sense? What parts of the story were enjoyable and why?
- ❏ Ask students to write a program summary describing a video they have seen. Include the title, actors, a short description of the story, and some drawings that illustrate the theme of the video.
- ❏ Have students compose an imaginary telegram

describing a video in five sentences. Then have them write another telegram describing the same video using only two sentences.
- Together with students, outline a sequel to a video, including these elements: plot (a series of events with a beginning, middle, and ending or resolution), characters, setting (time in history, time of year, time of day, and place), conflict, resolution, and theme—the overall message of the story.
- Ask the children to choose a video that interests them and to create something that captures a moment from the video and portrays it visually. Provide them with a variety of materials so they can draw, paint, sculpt, make collages, or a combination of these.

Plot

- It has been said that every story ever told or written fits into one of four basic plots: (1) one character against another, (2) a character against nature, (3) a character against society, or (4) a character struggling with his or her own inner values. After discussing each of the four basic plots, ask the class to brainstorm fairy tales and discuss which type of plot each has. Then do the same exercise using video stories or movies seen by students in the class. Do any stories fit in more than one category? Does this formula help us to understand plots? Why or why not?
- Have students imagine that they are producers and that they have the power to change one aspect of a story. What part would they change? How would that change the outcome of the story?
- With students, list all of the videos they can remember that have the following plot elements: someone has a huge task to accomplish, a hero/heroine learns great things from an older person, a protagonist wishes for a more exciting life, a character must find three objects or accomplish

three tasks, or one of the characters defeats some sort of monster. See what comparisons can be made in each category. What other categories are there?
- With students, compare two plots of similar videos seen recently by the class. Which plot is more complex and why? Does the complexity make the video more enjoyable? Why or why not?
- Use role playing as a way to interpret a video. Pick one or two characters and have children act out specific parts of the video, adding their own creative flair to the parts.

Character

- Writers create believable characters by showing (1) what the character says and does, (2) what other people in the story say or think about the character, and (3) how other people in the story act toward the character. Select a character from a video to analyze with the class. Write the three methods on the blackboard and then ask students to give concrete examples from the video for each method.
- Brainstorm with the class characters they have met in videos—animated or live action. Fill the chalkboard with the characters' names. Is there any character they would like to know in real life? (Emphasize the character versus the movie star.) Suggest to the class that they imagine they can spend a Saturday with the character of their choice. How would they spend their time together? What would they talk about? Would they bring along a friend, or would they want to be alone with the character? Why?
- Choose a student to interview the main character from a video about a famous person. Role-play an important press conference. Encourage the interviewer to ask who, what, when, where, why, and how questions.

- Suggest students write a riddle, rhyme, or limerick about a main character in a video and read it to the class.
- Instruct students to write the names of characters from a variety of video stories on the left-hand side of a piece of paper. On the right-hand side, have them write questions that would be fun or interesting to pose to each character.

Character Interaction

- In a video showing family life, invite students to note when characters are nice to each other, laugh, compliment one another, or congratulate someone. How does the other person respond to this positive interaction? Show the video again, and this time have students note when characters are not nice to one another. Note when someone argues, hits, provokes, or laughs at another character. Again, how does the other character react? Is the reaction hostile or antagonistic, or does the character react to put-downs by doing something mean in return? How else could the character have gotten his or her point of view across to the other person? Why do characters in TV situation comedies yell at each other so much?
- Challenge children to imagine how two well-known characters from different videos might interact with each other. Have the students invent a story in which Bilbo Baggins from *The Hobbit* finds himself picnicking in the sunshine with Beth or Jo from *Little Women,* or Huck Finn is spending time with Chuck Yeager, the test pilot from *The Right Stuff.*

Actions, Decision Making, and Motivation

- Talk about characters in videos who have made significant decisions. How did they come to decide

Understanding the Story 55

what to do? Ask students what they think of particular decisions. How would they have handled the same situations?

- In order to help students synthesize and thus understand how a character's actions affect the story, ask questions such as, "Suppose [name of character] had not done [action taken by the character] but had done [another action] instead; what might have happened?" Have students write a sequel to the story built around another type of action taken by the character.
- Talk about the main character in a video. Did this person have a dilemma? What was it? What possible action could he or she have taken? What would be the consequences of this course of action? What solution did the character choose? How else could the dilemma have been solved? Discuss and list on the chalkboard additional solutions to the problem.
- People have many different kinds of needs. Everyone needs food, clothing, and shelter, but people have additional needs as well—the needs to achieve, to be liked, to be respected, and to be accepted, to name just a few. Identify a video with a character who makes his or her needs known. How are those needs discussed or demonstrated? How do the people around the character respond? Are the needs met?
- Identify a video that has characters who have personal problems. What are the problems? How were the problems handled? Ask students if they would have handled the problems differently. How or why not?
- With students, identify stories that describe a character's quest. What is the purpose of such stories? These stories usually take place in the past or the future, not the present. Is this always the case?
- Ask children to imagine that a character from a video who was in a jam was given magical powers. How would this change the story?

Feelings about Characters

- Ask individual students to identify characters they like from recently seen videos, and ones that they do not like. Why? What do characters do to make students like or dislike them? Ask other class members if they agree or disagree with the speaker's opinion. Discuss what motivates the character to act in a certain way.
- Discuss what influences the way the audience feels about a character in a video. Is the audience supposed to sympathize with a character? Are they supposed to like or dislike the character? How else might a filmmaker want the viewer to feel about a character? Ask students if they have ever changed the way they felt about a character in the course of watching a video. Ask them to name people they have met in books that they felt strongly about, either liking or disliking. Discuss why the characters evoked such strong reactions.
- Discuss first impressions. How does the class feel about a character in the beginning of a video? Stop the VCR and take a show of hands as to first impressions: those who like or trust or respect a character versus those who do not like or trust or respect the character. Later on in the story, when they have had an opportunity to get to know the character, how do they feel about him or her?
- Ask students to identify a likable character in a video. What did the character do to make the viewer like him or her? How do the other characters in the video feel about the one who has been identified as being likable?
- With students, identify a disagreeable character in a video. What did the character do to make the audience not like him or her? How do the other characters in the video feel about the one who has been identified as being disagreeable?

Understanding the Story 57

- Ask students if they have met a character in a video whose actions they respected. What did the character do? Was it difficult? If they or a friend had done what the character did, would they have felt proud? Did anyone in the story support this character? Did anyone oppose the character?
- With students, identify characters in videos whose behavior would have embarrassed the students if they or a friend had done what the character had done. Why?

Character Traits and Personalities

- Compare characters from two different videos who have similar personalities, such as Natty in *The Journey of Natty Gann* and Kate in *Starlight Hotel*. Describe each girl's personality. What makes her tick? How does she feel about the people in her life and herself? How are the two girls similar? How are they different? Whose character is more developed? How is this shown? Does this affect the overall story?
- Discuss character assets and flaws. Identify characters who demonstrate such traits as kindness, love of friends, and tolerance. Then identify characters who demonstrate traits such as selfishness, greed, and lack of sensitivity. What are the repercussions of each character's actions?
- Write the names of characters from a video on index cards and tape the names on students' backs. Have each student figure out whose name is on his or her back by asking classmates questions about the character. Which questions are useful, and which are not?
- Have students make a list of positive words describing people, such as *truthful, wise,* and *responsible.* Then have them make a list of words with negative connotations, such as *foolish, mean, and dishonest.* As the class watches a video, have

them list words that describe a character's personality as they are demonstrated in the video. Then have students draw a family crest for one of the characters, using pictures to illustrate the person's qualities.

Heroes, Heroines, and Villains

- Discuss what a hero or heroine is (see Glossary). Ask students what they think the word *hero* means, who some of their heroes are, and perhaps who their parents look up to as heroes. What does someone have to do to be considered a hero? Do authorities consider people such as pop stars to be heroes? Identify heroes of old. Who is alive today who might someday be considered a hero? Look up the dictionary definition of *hero*. (Note: You may find it interesting to refer to a conversation between historian Barbara Tuchman and Bill Moyers in Moyers's book *The World of Ideas*. Tuchman talks about the true meaning of *hero*: "One of the attributes of a hero, apart from being originally half-mortal and half-divine and performing deeds of valor, is nobility of purpose." This discussion is available on video in *The National Soul: Myth, Morality and Ethics in the American Consciousness* [Mystic Fire Video]. After you have discussed the concept of the hero fully, you might locate this short segment in the conversation to show your class.)
- Now that your students know the true meaning of *hero*, brainstorm with them to identify real people with "nobility of purpose." Are there video biographies about any of them? Encourage your class to write to producers, requesting that they consider producing tapes on one of these real-life heroes.
- Have the children think about their favorite heroes/heroines. Then have them draw pedestals, topping

them with their heroes/heroines doing something symbolic of their talents. The children can show their pictures to the class and have other students guess the identity of the character on the pedestal.
- After seeing a video about one of our national heroes, have the children draw the hero's picture as it might appear on the cover of a magazine, using felt-tip markers or water paints.
- Ask students to identify villains or evil characters in the videos they have seen. What does *evil* mean? Why is someone evil? Was there one reason or many reasons that the person was evil? See if students can break down the character's evil to learn what caused it. How does the filmmaker manipulate the villain so that the audience does not sympathize with the character?

Setting

- Point out to students that the video's setting includes when the story takes place in history, the season, and the time of day or night, as well as the place. How does the viewer learn this information? Is the setting familiar to the viewer? If it is familiar, does this familiarity influence the feelings the viewer forms about the video?
- Research an unfamiliar town or city that is the setting for a story in a video. Find it on a map. What can be learned about it? Encourage the class to write to the town's Chamber of Commerce or tourist office, requesting information about the city, including maps, information about any nearby state or national parks, the kinds of recreational activities that are available, and the number of books in the library. Have students compare the size of their town with the researched town. What other information can the Chamber of Commerce or tourist office provide that would be of interest?

- ❏ Discuss the setting of a video. Are clues given that help viewers identify the region where the story takes place? Do the characters use any special accents or idiomatic expressions that help viewers identify the story's setting? Does the period have a name, such as the Victorian era? Research the period.
- ❏ Have students make a diorama of a video's setting and characters, being sure to include clues as to the time in history and time of year. Suggest that they provide thought bubbles over the characters' heads indicating important points in the story.

Conflict

- ❏ Many videos are stories with conflict that needs to be resolved. Discuss why conflict is necessary in a story. Have the children identify conflict in stories they have read. How do they identify conflict? Is it always violent? How is it resolved in the story? Form groups and agree upon a point of conflict in a story for a discussion. Have students discuss how the conflict was created and then act it out.
- ❏ Have students evaluate the plots of several fairy tales (such as "Goldilocks and the Three Bears," "Little Red Riding Hood," "Beauty and the Beast"), looking at the element of conflict. How does conflict or a problem help to shape each story?

Theme

- ❏ It is usually easy to identify the plot in a well-written story, but it is sometimes more difficult to spot the theme. Discuss with children the themes in recently seen videos about friendship, self-reliance, growing up, or initiative.

Technical Style

Language

- In order to direct children's attention to how writers use words, explain that you are going to read to them the nursery rhyme "The Gingerbread Man." Tell the children that you would like them to think about what preschoolers might enjoy about this story. Notice that repetition is used to build a rhythm in the narration. There is something very satisfying about the patterns. What other stories use rhythm in this way?
- The story of "The Gingerbread Man" engages very young children by using repetition and a little character who outwits lots of people. Why might some children feel unsatisfied by the Gingerbread Man's demise? Encourage the class to create another ending.
- From a book that you especially enjoy, read a passage aloud for its richness of style. An example might be a segment from *Charlotte's Web*, *Treasure Island*, *Mrs. Frisby and the Rats of NIMH*, *The Jungle Book*, or *Tuck Everlasting*. Discuss with the class the author's use of language. Identify other authors who make good use of language.
- Listen to an audiotape in a foreign language. How does it sound? Have the class clap to its rhythm. Can the students understand any of it? What do they know about the people who speak this language? Are their observations based on stereotypes, or on actual people they know who demonstrate the behaviors the students have identified?

Tragedy

- Discuss with the class what a tragedy is (see Glossary). What are some stories that are considered to be tragedies? Identify characters whose lives would be considered tragic. If you are good, you deserve good, but in tragedies bad things happen to good people. Does it seem fair that this should happen? What does *fair* mean?

Violence

- Discuss the role violence plays in videos. Watch a video that has a fight scene. Have students list the sound effects, props, special effects, and makeup used to create the feeling of reality. How does an audience react to violence?
- Identify the violent elements in the videos students have seen and discuss why the violence was present. Is violence always a necessary story component or is it sometimes a device to keep the action moving?

Flashbacks

- Present the concept of flashbacks in video. Find videos that use this technique to tell a story. Ask for a student volunteer to tell a short story using flashback episodes. Taking an example from a recently viewed video, ask if anyone can put the sequence of events in chronological order. Have students retell the story sequentially.

Humor

- Everyone loves a funny story. Discuss with children the humorous elements in a video they have just watched. What is it that makes the story funny? Does everyone laugh in the same places? Why or why not? Was it a comedy? Why? Why not? What are the topics or skits that seem to have universal human appeal?
- Show any five minutes of *City Lights* or another Charlie Chaplin film. Identify where your class laughs in those five minutes. Ask a teacher from

a different grade level to do the same thing, and share the results with your class. Discuss with your class where they laughed and where children from another grade laughed. Ask the children what they make of this.
- Suggest to students that they observe members of their family while watching a situation comedy on television to learn what kinds of things make each of them laugh. Can any conclusions be formed?

Point of View
- To explain that some documentaries have specific points of view, first show one and then divide the class into three groups to retell it. One group retells it with an objective point of view, one group looks at the positive aspects of the story, and the third group looks at the negative side of the story. Have the students present and discuss their differing points of view.

Sensory Information
- Some stories arouse the senses: sight, hearing, smell, touch, and/or taste. One way for an animator or storyteller to engage an audience is to evoke the senses in the story. Ask students to identify when a sense has been used in this way.

Understanding Video Production Techniques

- Send students to the library to research all areas of video production: live action, animation, sets, acting, roles. Have them report back to the class with what they have learned.
- Ask students to pretend they have won a trip to a Hollywood movie studio. Suggest that they brainstorm questions to use when interviewing

producers, actors, directors, and technical people. Encourage students to think up probing questions that require thoughtful answers.
- It takes considerable teamwork to produce a video. Have children carefully watch the opening and closing credits of a video. List each job and appoint a committee to research what each person's job entails.

ACTING

- Point out to students that although acting might look simple, it is a demanding profession that requires skill, determination, and talent. How and why do people become actors? What skills are involved in acting?
- Perhaps you or one of your students knows a professional actor who would be willing to visit the class and talk about the craft of acting. Or you could call a local theater company or actors' guild to see if a member would be interested in talking to the class.
- Discuss the word *respect*. What does someone do to earn other people's respect? Who are people from the past who deserve respect? Poll the class to learn who their most respected actors and actresses are. Why is each respected? Record the responses on a graph.
- Ask the children what parts they would like to play in a certain story and have them explain why. Have them draw themselves in scenes with some of the other characters in the video.
- Have students consider the quality of acting in a video by asking themselves the following questions about each character: Was the actor/actress believable? Was he or she right for the part? Did the viewer care about the actor or actress? Were his or her voice, facial expressions, physical features, age, stance, and walk well suited to the role? Did the character have an identifiable idiosyncrasy? If

Understanding Video Production Techniques

so, was it appropriate for the role? Why or why not? Did the actors and actresses work well together? How could the viewer tell?
- Sometimes actors in movies and videos are able to do things that real people cannot do. Discuss a video in which the hero or heroine did something that is not humanly possible. How was the action performed? Were costumes, makeup, props, or special effects used to enhance the featured character?
- Sometimes it is possible to understand what another person is thinking about by watching for nonverbal cues or messages. Watch a video with students and focus on the actors' body language. How do the actors convey thoughts and feelings by the way they move, sit, walk, and so on?

ANIMATION

- Students are interested in learning about how animation is done. Send a committee to the library to research clay animation, cell animation, and line, cutout, and silhouette animation. Discuss why an animator chooses one form of animation over another. Select several videos that use various animation techniques and see if the students can identify them. Perhaps the school's art department could coordinate a unit on animation for your class.
- Children enjoy making their own flip books. Small white scratch pads from the five-and-ten work well because the paper is thin. Show the class a basic flip book (these can be purchased at many stationery or specialty stores for a couple of dollars, or you can make your own to use as a demonstration). Discuss how the effect of movement was created. Have the children plan the movements they want in their flip books, such as a flower blooming, a child waving, or a person jumping. After they have planned what to draw, the students can begin their books. Using felt-tip pens, the students draw on the

last page of the pad, then lay the next-to-last page over it and redraw the picture, changing it slightly in the direction of the desired movement; they continue in this manner until the movement being pictured is complete. Then, by turning to the last page of the book and flipping the pages as they go toward the front, the students can see their own animation.
- Children can make their own films by a simple process. Locate clear or white 16mm film leader and demonstrate how to create homemade films. First, put white paper over the surface where film is to be placed and tape down several feet of film leader, depending on the number of children involved in the activity. Have students draw on the side of the film that is more absorbent, using felt-tip pens. Suggest to the class that they think of the film as a long piece of paper to decorate. Explain that one second of film is equal to 24 frames. Each drawing is shown twice, so in order to see a flower for one second, the flower must be drawn 12 times.

CAMERA WORK

- Discuss the vocabulary specific to camera work: pan, close-up, head shot, zoom in, and zoom out. When the camera is tilted up, the image looks different from when the camera is positioned straight on or tilted down. Long shots have effects that are different from those of close-ups. Zooming in with the camera is different from zooming out. If possible, locate a video camera and allow children to look through it and experiment with different kinds of shots, discussing the strengths of each.
- Show the class a short video that demonstrates different camera angles. Show the video a second time, and have them call out each camera technique as it is used.

Understanding Video Production Techniques 67

- Point out that the way a shot looks depends on the position of the camera. If the camera is pointed straight ahead, the shot will look normal. Tilting the camera up or down will make the image look distorted. Ask students to draw a character from a video three times, each from a different point of view: once with a straight shot, once as if the camera were tilted up to make the character look large, and once as if the camera were tilted down to make the character look small.
- A camera can zoom in on a person for a close-up, also called a head shot. To make an object appear far away, the camera zooms out, giving a full top-to-bottom shot. Have students draw two pictures of a favorite villain, "zooming in" for a head shot in the first drawing, then "zooming out" for a top-to-bottom shot in the second.
- Comic strips provide an excellent vehicle for explaining point of view. Collect enough comics for each student to have a complete story (usually four frames). Direct the children to look at each frame and consider how a camera would have to be positioned to "shoot" the picture in the frame.
- Discuss what effect a camera shot has on the viewer's interpretation of the story. How does the position of the camera affect the telling of the story? How would a shot taken from a child's point of view differ from the same shot taken from an adult's point of view? For instance, how might a camera show a child brushing her teeth as opposed to showing an adult brushing his teeth?
- Discuss books, videos, and films that make use of unusual illustrations and camera work to communicate a point of view. Have students look through picture books for examples.
- Videos of symphony orchestras provide excellent opportunities to see interesting camera techniques, as the camera alternately captures the instruments, the players, the conductor, and the audience

enjoying the concert. There are many wonderful tapes available of superb orchestras. Select a short segment or two to show the class and discuss the different ways the camera is used.
- Discuss how camera angle affects a viewer's emotional reaction to a scene. For example, a director may cause the camera to be positioned differently in order to achieve a sense of superiority, smallness, or importance. Instruct the class to organize a shooting of the following scenarios: (1) The principal sends for a student who is to be congratulated for making the honor roll. How might the camera be positioned to enhance the viewer's respect for the student? (2) The principal reprimands a student for carelessly breaking a window. How might the camera be positioned to create a feeling of sympathy for the student?
- Discuss how a director might position the camera so the audience does not like a character. How would the director instruct the actor to behave? What type of expressions would be effective in influencing the audience's feelings for the character?

COLOR VERSUS BLACK-AND-WHITE PHOTOGRAPHY

- Have students close their eyes and imagine the world in black and white. Ask them to imagine a sunset, their favorite football player making a touchdown, a rainbow above a field of daisies, or a fancy restaurant filled with people and food. Following the screening of a black-and-white video, do an image-sound skim (see Glossary) with the students. Discuss the differences in images when viewing in black and white versus color.
- Turn off the color on your set or monitor and discuss the changes brought on by eliminating color. When does black and white enhance a video? Why? Some black-and-white videos are having

Understanding Video Production Techniques

color added to them. Why would some producers and directors not want old films to be colorized? Why would some people want black-and-white films to be colorized?

COSTUMES AND SCENERY

- Discuss why costumes and makeup are important in a video program. Have children think about how the actors and actresses were dressed in a recently seen video. Ask them to consider the effect the costumes attempted to achieve. Did this effect enhance the video? Ask students what they did and did not like about how a particular character was dressed. Have the students draw any costume as it appeared in the video, and then have them draw their ideas for a different costume for the same character.
- A costume can tell a great deal about a character's age and position in life. What else do costumes tell about a person? In dramatic productions, costumes help to set the tone of the story. Have students describe the main character's costume in a video they have recently seen. What does it tell about the story and about this character in the story? Is the costume appropriate for this character? Why or why not?
- Sets are designed according to specific instructions given to the set designer by the production team. Discuss the type of information a set conveys about a story. Have students draw a room set or a scene that has been shot outdoors. Ask students to draw an original set for a video.

EDITING

- Editing is a process that older children find very interesting. Plan a visit to a local television station, where students can see how a television production is put together, especially the final editing.

PRODUCTION VALUES

- Ask students to think about their favorite films or videos. What makes them successful in terms of the quality of the production? What aspects of the production hold their attention and why? To determine the quality of a program, consider the camera work, lighting, direction of the actors and actresses, costumes, makeup, and the set. Why are production values important to consider when talking about videos?
- Talk about what you can learn about a producer by examining the videos that he or she has produced. Look at the work of Joshua Greene (Stories To Remember series, *Choosing the Best in Children's Video; What's a Good Story? Beauty and the Beast*) and Tom Davenport (*Ashpet: An American Cinderella; Hansel and Gretel; Jack and the Dentist's Daughter*). Have students write a letter to a producer asking about his or her work. Suggest that they include such questions as, What does a producer do? What was it about producing that seemed interesting or appealing? What does he or she enjoy about producing? What does he or she find difficult? Was it necessary to take special courses to become a producer? What special skills or knowledge are needed to become a producer?

SCRIPTING AND STORYBOARDING

- Photographs and films tell stories in similar ways. In order to prepare a storyboard for a video, ask each student to bring in a favorite photograph. Look at the photograph and identify four different shots in it. For example, in a picture of three children watching a man drawing, the shots could include a close-up of the man's hand, then a shot of one of the children, a shot of the man's face, and then a full shot of the entire group. Provide the class with paper to draw their four different shots. Encourage them to consider the dialogue as well as the music and sound effects that would accompany the scene.

From *Squiggles, Dots and Lines*. Photo courtesy of KIDVIDZ.

- ❏ Children enjoy reading scripts. Point out that all productions in television, film, and video use scripts. Well-written dialogue is an important component of any story. Have students work in small groups to develop and write a script for a short story.

SOUND

- ❏ Watch a video for 60 seconds with the sound turned off. Then for the next 60 seconds, turn

Video Activities: Fourth through Sixth Grade

the sound on and the picture off. Compare and contrast the two experiences. What is missed? Is anything gained?
- Talk about how music is used in videos. Ask students to note when music is used in a dramatic video. Is the music just background or does it perform a function? Often music is used as a warning to prepare the audience for something that is about to happen. How else is music used?
- Have children imagine a video they have recently watched as a radio show. What sound effects would be necessary to make it effective? Would the same actors/actresses be successful on radio? Whose voices would work for the lead roles?
- Instruct the class to organize a ten-minute radio program. They must think about the type of show it will be (news, interview, music, sports event, short story), the specific content of the show, and the types of sound effects they will need to make the program more interesting. Have them assign different people to write the script, to collect the items to create the sound effects, and to record the actual program. Play the finished program back to the class for comments.
- Many television programs have laugh tracks (see Glossary). Discuss the purpose of a laugh track. Do any videos have laugh tracks? Why or why not?

SPECIAL EFFECTS
- Often children comment during a video, "That couldn't really happen!" Discuss why some truly unbelievable things can happen in videos because of special effects.
- Ask students for examples of films and videos that use special effects. Discuss how the videos would be different if special effects were not used.
- Conduct a survey to find out what kinds of special effects are preferred by children in different age

groups. Each child might ask preschoolers, first graders, third graders, eighth graders, high school students, college students, and his or her own parents to name the videos they like, keeping track of what videos are liked by each age group. From students' lists, determine the types of special effects, if any, used in each video. Have students create graphs showing their findings. Can any generalizations be made from the findings?
- Suggest that the class produce a video that answers often-asked questions. Each child is responsible for three minutes of the video. Have each student choose a question to research, such as why we need to take care of the planet's resources, why humans float in water, or why the game of football has four quarters. After they find the answers, give students paper or cards to create storyboards for the segments of the video that answer their questions.

SPECIAL TECHNOLOGY

- Closed captions offer nonhearing people an entry to television. With a closed-caption decoder, the dialogue appears in subtitles on the bottom of the screen. These subtitles are much like those seen in foreign films. The decoder has other uses, too. Discuss with students some ways to use this piece of technology to help people who are learning English as a second language.
- The decoder is also useful for encouraging people to read. If possible, borrow a decoder and locate a video with closed captions. Watch the program with the class, noting any mistakes in spelling and syntax. Now find a program on television with closed captions and watch it together, again noting any spelling mistakes and problems of syntax. Is the program live or prerecorded? Does this make a difference?
- Ask for a volunteer or volunteers to research more

about closed captions and report back to the class. (See Appendix B for the address of the National Captioning Institute.) How is it done? When a show on TV is live, what happens to the captions?

USING THE VCR

- In order to work with video, students need to know how to use the VCR, too. Instruct and/or review with the class the correct way to insert a tape, start a tape by pushing the "play" button, fast forward, reverse, and pause a tape, as well as how and when to use the counter.
- With students' help, review the proper care of videocassettes and the importance of clearly labeling what is on each cassette.
- VCRs are delicate machines, and they need careful attention. Discuss the care that VCRs need to work efficiently, such as protection from dust and water, and proper storage.

VIDEO PRODUCTION ACTIVITIES

- Have the class present a dramatic reading of a short story that has a video adaptation (preferably one that no one in the class has seen). The children decide what the script should include, who will say what, and how to introduce the story to capture the audience's attention. Tape the reading and play it back, emphasizing what the students learned from creating the dramatic reading. Schedule a viewing time to see the adaptation and then compare and contrast the class's reading with the video adaptation.
- To produce three-minute videos, form small groups and ask each group to select a short poem to present. With each group, discuss why they chose a specific poem and how their choice will work for a reading on video. Each group will need a producer (responsible for the entire production), a camera

operator, and talent (the people who appear on camera). For this type of production, head shots work well because the camera focuses on one student and there is no need for costumes or a set. Have students write the script, choose parts, and practice. They are now ready to shoot the poetry reading. "Lights, camera, action!"

- Produce a five-minute show reviewing five tapes about a particular topic, such as the environment, health, sports, or the Civil War. See Appendix A for suggestions.
- Suggest to the children that they create a show called "Video Rainbow," like "Reading Rainbow," the Public Broadcasting television program. One part will include summaries of great videos, much like the summaries of books done by and for kids on "Reading Rainbow." In order to create an outline for "Video Rainbow," students will need to learn what information is included in the "Read All about It" segment on "Reading Rainbow." Watch this segment from several programs. What information is given about each book? Would it be useful to provide this same information for videos? What else would a viewer want to know about videos? How do the reviewers present their material? Analyze "Read All about It" and put together an outline to be used for creating the segment for "Video Rainbow." Select videos to be included and get ready for the camera to roll.
- An overhead projector and transparencies provide a good opportunity for students to write and illustrate a story. After students write their stories, have them practice illustrating the stories on 8½-by-11-inch sheets of paper. When they are satisfied with their illustrations, have them draw on transparencies with permanent felt-tip markers. Clear tape will hold the plastic transparencies together as each student narrates his or her story while moving the plastic sheets across the screen.

Using Video To Build Skills, Knowledge, and Understanding

BOOKS AND VIDEO

- After reading a descriptive passage from a children's book, discuss how the passage might be translated into a visual medium such as video. How could it be shown visually? Discuss whether or not the video could capture the writer's meaning. What are the strengths and/or weaknesses of books adapted to video? What has worked and what has not? Why are so many videos adaptations of books? Whenever possible, have students give concrete examples to back up their opinions.
- Since 1938, illustrators of the most distinguished children's picture books published in America have been awarded the Caldecott Medal. Locate a list of books that have won this award (available from the American Library Association). How many of the books have been read by each student? Discuss the Caldecott winners that have been adapted to video. Choose one or more of the books to read aloud to the class; after reading a book, show its video adaptation.
- Since 1922, the Newbery Medal has been presented annually to the authors of the best American children's literature. Locate a list of books that have won this award (available from the American Library Association). Explaining that these are books written for younger children, ask how many of the books have been read by each student. Discuss the books that have been adapted to video.
- Brainstorm and list the titles of books that have been read by the class. Ask the children to describe the qualities that make each book appealing. Encourage them to discuss plot, characterization, setting, and the conflict or problem that must be solved in order for the story to be resolved.

Using Video To Build Skills, Knowledge, Understanding

- Younger children enjoy working with older ones on special projects. Ask for volunteers to read a book and show the video adaptation to a group of younger children. The volunteers should practice reading the book, locate the video adaptation, and prepare three questions about the book and video to discuss with the children.

EXPLORING EMOTIONS

- Before watching a particularly poignant video, ask the children to name as many different feelings as they can. List them on the chalkboard. Before you show the video, ask the class to draw a "here-and-now wheel" on a piece of paper (see Glossary). At significant moments during the video, ask them to note their feelings on a spoke of their wheels. (It might be useful for you to note the VCR counter number each time you do this, so you will be able to fast forward to these segments for review.) After viewing the video, discuss each moment and ask for volunteers to share their notations about it.
- Ask children to suggest different emotions and list them on the chalkboard—love, hate, fear, anger, sadness, frustration, stubbornness, and so on. Discuss and list tapes that show emotion, beginning with tapes for young children and working up to tapes appropriate for the class. Divide the class into groups and ask them to isolate segments within tapes that demonstrate specific emotions. Ask each group to share three of their findings. The children will need to (1) identify the emotion, (2) locate a segment in a tape demonstrating the emotion, and (3) cue up the tape at the segment in order to show it to the class.
- After watching a video that deals with emotional issues, give each child a piece of paper. Ask them to draw a here-and-now wheel, and suggest that

they write specific feelings that the video evoked in the spokes of the wheel. Ask volunteers to share their feelings with the group.

EXPLORING VALUES

- Discuss "society's values" with students. Ask students to suggest values that are respected in their families, school, peer group, or church or synagogue, such as freedom, responsibility, respect for others, loyalty, obedience, self-control, courage, honesty, self-respect, self-discipline, inquisitiveness, self-reliance, justice, equality, and initiative. Have they observed characters in videos who demonstrate any of these qualities? Have any characters challenged these values? Can a character's actions demonstrate too much of a value so that it gets in his or her way? What values do students personally honor?

PREJUDICE AND STEREOTYPES

- After watching a video, discuss the word *prejudice*—to prejudge. Look it up in the dictionary. Discuss what might motivate someone to be prejudiced. Ask students if any characters in the video exhibited a prejudice. Do they know of anyone on TV or in videos with identifiable prejudices?
- Have students look for stereotypes in advertisements for feature films in the local newspapers, especially photographs that are exploitive. What techniques are used in advertisements to persuade people to attend a movie? Do the advertisements succeed in influencing people to buy movie tickets? Ask students to write an ad for a film they have seen.

LANGUAGE, SPEAKING, AND WRITING SKILLS

- Ask a child to volunteer as a video discussion leader.

Plan a time when the child can view a video and make up possible questions and activities to be used before and after a class viewing. Have the discussion leader choose the next student to be the leader.

- With students, identify idiomatic expressions used in a video. Research their origins. Have students draw pictures that literally interpret the idiomatic expressions.
- What does it mean to say, "That's a profound statement"? Discuss profound observations made by any students in your class and then ask them to consider if a character in a video has said anything profound. Have students think about a favorite character and create a profound statement that he or she might say, making sure that it is believable that the character would make that observation.
- It is interesting to track how much of a person's conversation is fact and how much is opinion. On pieces of paper, have students draw one wide column and two narrow ones. Label the two narrow columns "fact" and "opinion." Watch a video and have students follow one character's conversation during a video, listing the statements in the first column and checking either the fact or the opinion column to indicate what each statement is. At the end of the video, count up the checks in each column and discuss the results.
- Discuss journal writing and the kinds of entries that students might make: what happened at school, something about a classmate, a weekend trip with the family. Have students select a character from a video and write an entry in a journal for a special day in this person's life—birthday, first day of school, first trip on an airplane. Talk about the "voice" that the writer will give to the character in the journal entry. Is there a way the entry can be written to make it sound like the voice of the character in the video?

- Have students keep video journals. After seeing a video, but before any class discussion, ask students to make entries in their journals. The content and form of entries are up to them—key words, thoughts, images, and phrases from the video to explore later; poems; reactions to a character or to the plot. The point is to encourage the children to write in order to pull together their ideas so that they will be ready to take part in the class discussion.
- Have the class adapt a video to a poem or play and present it to another class.
- Instruct students to create a 30-second sales pitch for a video in order to convince the principal to see it or to convince the principal that it should be shown to the school. Then ask students to select a video that they did not like, think about why someone might like it, and make a sales pitch for it.
- This is a two-day project on the use of language. On the first day, read to the class a passage from a book or story of your choice that demonstrates superb use of language and that has been adapted to video. Encourage students to be active listeners. The second day, elicit comments from students pertaining to the author's use of words. Then show the video adaptation to the class, following the viewing with more discussion of language.

MEDIA AWARENESS

- Ask students to list the ways that video, film, and TV influence or change people's points of view on topics such as the importance of clothes in people's lives, morality, and war. The discussion might include thoughts concerning television coverage of the daily news and the impact of commercials.
- Have students find movie advertisements in the local newspaper and use a highlighter to pick out

all the adjectives that are used to describe a film. List the adjectives on the chalkboard. Do the movie advertisements always describe a film correctly?
- ❏ Ask children to list the television shows and videos they have seen in the past week. Encourage them to look for patterns in their viewing habits. Is their viewing menu balanced, including both nonfiction and fiction, live-action and animated shows? How much TV and video are they watching each day? What other activities do they enjoy? What do they do while they are watching TV or video? How much do they remember about a program that they watched last week? What did they learn from it? Was it a good way to spend time? Why or why not? Query the class as to other questions they might ask in order to scrutinize their viewing habits.
- ❏ Children frequently choose to watch television in their free time. While watching TV, they are not exploring other activities. Make a list of activities children might enjoy pursuing if their television sets were broken for a month or if there were twice as much time as is currently available.
- ❏ Discuss the types of television programs, videos, and films that students consider a waste of time. Encourage them to think about why poor-quality programs are produced and presented to the public. Is there anything they can do to voice their opinions to the television stations?
- ❏ As a class project, have students write letters to video distributors or manufacturers suggesting the type of programming that appeals to young people ages 9 to 12. Encourage the children to name a few of their favorite videos in the letters in order to give the distributors a clear picture of the type of programming they enjoy.

Evaluating Videos
- ❏ Reviews evaluate products such as books, TV shows,

movies, and videos so that consumers may make educated decisions about what to read or watch. Explain what kind of information is included in reviews: comments on plot, story logic, theme, casting, acting, makeup, costumes, music, and special effects. Read some reviews to the class and discuss whether the reviewers covered the necessary information.

- What is meant by the statement, "Reviewers often have a strong point of view"? Collect reviews from local newspapers and magazines and have students analyze each writer's point of view.
- Survey students to learn the names of recent films they have attended. Collect articles reviewing these movies and read them to the class. Ask students whether they agree or disagree with the film reviewer's point of view and why.
- Have the class create a newspaper and include a section that reviews videos. Review the elements of a production that a film or video critic considers important to include in a review—the quality of the acting and/or animation, costumes, camera work, lighting, music, and special effects, if any.
- After showing them a video containing new information, encourage the children to evaluate what they learned from it. Did the director and producer use any teaching techniques? How else might the viewer obtain the same information? Is video the best way to learn that specific information? Why or why not? What type of information would be best learned from books? From video? From both?
- Break the class into small groups, and ask each group to designate a person to do the writing. Instruct the groups to write the names of 20 videos on 20 separate 3-by-5-inch index cards, then spread the cards out and consider ways to group them—live action, animation, nonfiction, fiction, animals, musicals, fine arts, adaptations of books, biography, science fiction, how-to, coming-of-age, and so on.

How many different categories come to mind? Have each group's writer note on the back of each card the category it is in. Then have the groups shuffle the cards and distribute them into different groups, again noting categories on the backs of the cards. Do the exercise a third time. Encourage groups to discuss why they are placing each video in a specific category.

Impact of Video and Television on Our Life-Styles

❑ Discuss the ways video and television have influenced our life-styles. Perhaps videos have shown children some new and interesting facts or how to do something, such as a hobby, that they might not have contemplated before. List with the students the positive and negative influences of viewing videos.

Evaluating Video for Specific Ages

❑ In order to point out that children relate to media differently depending on their age, explain that very young children (below ages 5 or 6) believe what they see and may think that the characters live in the monitor. Explain that your students are going to be critics who decide which of the many adaptations of a fairy tale is appropriate for a specific age group. Choose a fairy tale that has many adaptations (see Appendix A). Select one short scene from the fairy tale and show each adaptation's interpretation of that scene. Ask children to choose which would be appropriate for a 3-year-old, a 6-year-old, and an 8-year-old. (See Chapters Three and Seven for descriptions of each age group's media needs.)

❑ Explain that the class is responsible for the selection of three tapes for a child in nursery school to see this weekend. In order to make the selections, they need to know what is appropriate for 3–4-year-olds. Begin by asking the class to describe children of this age. What do they enjoy doing? What makes them laugh? What do they find frightening? It might be useful to write on the chalkboard "Activities," "Laughs at?" and "What's scary?" to help focus the discussion. Then elicit titles that would be appropriate for children in preschool.

❏ Have the class construct a ten-minute skit reviewing videos for children in kindergarten through third grade. In order to do this they will need to evaluate videos designed for young children. Have the class review fiction and nonfiction videos, including how-tos, and be sure to include both live-action and animated tapes. The class will select several tapes to review and will build the skit around them. The skit should include information about each tape's plot, characters, setting, and production quality. Be sure the skit does not give too much away—the audience should leave curious.

❏ Do the same project as above, only this time review videos for children in fourth through sixth grades.

SCIENCE AND SOCIAL STUDIES

❏ Identify science fiction movies produced in the 1950s and 1960s that made predictions about the future. Which predictions have come true? What has happened instead?

THINKING SKILLS

❏ Maurice Sendak, who is quoted at the front of this book, says, "I absolutely believe in the idea that things children are exposed to are laying down patterns in their brains. And so you can't read early enough to a child, you can't talk early enough to a child, you can't love early enough for a child, you can't bring music early enough into a child's life—it becomes part of the patterning."

Discuss what Sendak means by this statement. Ask students why this quote would be used in a book about using videos with children. Why would Sendak be a good source of quotes about children?

❑ Discuss what the word *communicate* means. What is the purpose of communication? How do people communicate with each other? Are humans the only animals who communicate? How do people who cannot hear communicate with others? Ask students if they have ever tried to tell someone something and felt the other person was not listening. Sometimes people talk at the same time. Why? Ask children to think of television shows or videos in which this has happened. How do the characters deal with it? What could they have done to get their messages across? Ask students if they have ever wanted to communicate something special to someone but were anxious about telling them. Did it help to plan out what they wanted to say? What happened if they just blurted out what was on their minds? Are there times when this works? Have students give examples from videos and television of the different methods.

86 Video Activities: Fourth through Sixth Grade

From *Jacob Have I Loved*. Photo courtesy of Public Media Video.

SIX

Connecting Activities with Specific Videos

In order to help you with the ongoing process of using video activities across the curriculum as a catalyst for thinking, this chapter describes how to connect activities with some specific video titles. Many, though not all, of these activities appear in Chapters Four and Five.

These descriptions are not meant to be prescriptive. Their purpose is to show how the ideas described in this book can serve as models for incorporating videos into lesson plans to enhance specific areas of the curriculum, to teach children to be more discriminating viewers, and to provide children with opportunities to refine their thinking skills. For information on distributors and suggested age recommendations for the video titles listed in the descriptions, see Appendix A.

Using Video To Understand and Appreciate Language and Literature

PURPOSE: TO EXPLORE
THE ELEMENTS OF A STORY

Grades: 4–6

Suggested Title: *Jacob Have I Loved*

Additional Titles To Consider: *Abe Lincoln: Freedom*

Fighter; Anne of Green Gables; Medicine Hat Stallion; Tuck Everlasting

Activity

After reading Katherine Paterson's book, but before seeing the video, divide the class into pairs and ask each pair to select a short segment from the story and plan a dramatic reading to present to the class.

The children decide what the script should include, who will say what, and how to introduce the story to capture the audience's attention. Audiotape the readings and play them back for the class, emphasizing what the students learned from preparing the dramatic readings, such as the importance of narration, timing, and sound effects.

After-Viewing Discussion

Discuss with the class the differences between the audio and video adaptations of the segments. (Note: It is best to view the video in more than one sitting. Children get far more from a lengthy production if they see it in smaller segments over more than one viewing. This also provides time for discussion.) Many themes and issues can be raised with students after they have watched the adaptation of Paterson's superb book. Using the activities as models, engage the class in a discussion about Louise and her twin sister, Caroline. These are complex characters who will provide fuel for provocative discussions.

Character Development

- Talk about characters in the video who made significant decisions. How did they come to decide what to do? What do you think of the decision? How would you have handled the same situation?
- Think about the main characters in the video. Did they have a dilemma? What was it? What

possible actions could they have taken? What are the possible consequences of each course of action? What solution did the character(s) choose? How else could the dilemma have been solved? Discuss and list on the chalkboard additional solutions to the problem.
- Have you ever wanted to communicate something special with someone but were anxious about telling them? Did it help to plan out what you wanted to say? What happened if you just blurted out what was on your mind? Are there times when this works? In *Jacob Have I Loved,* note Louise's actions toward the Captain. In her rage, she confronts him about the money he donated to Caroline's musical education. Discuss what she learns from the Captain. What do you think would have happened had she never gone to him? He says to her, "Find the one gift that is yours." How does Louise find her gift? Do you know any of your gifts?

Plot
- It has been said that all of the stories that have ever been told or written fit into one of four basic plots. Is *Jacob Have I Loved* a story about (1) one character against another, (2) a character against nature, (3) a character against society, or (4) a character struggling with her own inner values? After discussing each of the four basic plots, discuss which plot best sums up this video.
- Does this story fit into more than one plot category? Does the formula help us to understand plots? Why or why not?

Theme
- It is usually easy to identify the plot in a well-written story, but it is sometimes more difficult to spot the theme. Discuss with children the theme of *Jacob Have I Loved.*

Setting

- Both the book and the video evoke a very distinct sense of time and place—Chesapeake Island in the 1940s. Note: Refer to Chapter 6 in *Exploring Books with Gifted Children* by Polette and Hamlin (see Appendix C), in which the authors concentrate on the study of setting and mood and offer many excellent suggestions for facilitating discussion.
- Are clues given to help viewers identify the region where the story takes place? Are there any special accents, idiomatic expressions, or foods mentioned that help viewers to identify the time when the story takes place? Does the period have a name, such as the Victorian era? Ask for volunteers to research the period.

PURPOSE: TO EXPLORE CHARACTER DEVELOPMENT

Discussion Topic

A major difference between Saturday-morning cartoons and quality programming is the degree of character development. The more believable a character is, the more personality that is shown, the more likely the character is to be three-dimensional and well developed.

Grades: K–3

Suggested Title: *Really Rosie*

Additional Titles To Consider: *Madeline*; *Pippi Longstocking*; *Pollyanna*; "The Story about Ping" (in *The Story about Ping and Other Stories*)

Before-Viewing Discussion

Ask students to suggest well-developed characters from videos they have seen. What did the characters do that made them seem believable?

After-Viewing Discussion

How does Rosie show that she is a fully developed character?

Grades: 4–6

Suggested Titles: any in the WonderWorks series (see Appendix A)

Additional Titles To Consider: *The Black Stallion; The Boy Who Could Fly; Hockey Night; The Journey of Natty Gann; The Land of Faraway; Starlight Hotel; Tuck Everlasting; The Young Magician*

After-Viewing Discussion

The WonderWorks series (see Appendix A) features many multidimensional characters who experience growth during the course of the story. All of these titles have characters who would stimulate interesting class discussions about characterization. The following are just a few activities that would be good to use.

Character Development

- How does a production influence how the audience feels about a character? Is the audience supposed to sympathize with a character or like or dislike him or her? How else might a production want the viewer to feel about a character? Have you ever changed the way you felt about a character in the course of watching a video? Who are some people you have met in books or on the screen for whom you have felt strongly, either liking or disliking? Encourage students to think about and discuss why the character evoked this strong reaction.
- Talk about characters in videos who have made significant decisions. How did they come to decide what to do? What do students think of the decision and how would they have handled the situation?

92 Connecting Activities with Specific Videos

From *The Journey of Natty Gann*. Photo courtesy of Walt Disney Home Video.

PURPOSE: TO EXPLORE JOURNAL WRITING

Grades: 4–6

Suggested Titles: *Lassie Come Home; Little Women; National Velvet; Tuck Everlasting*

> Additional Titles To Consider: any in the Wonder-Works series

After-Viewing Discussion

Discuss the kinds of entries one might make in a journal. Select a character from a video and write an entry in a journal for special days in this person's life—birthday, first day of school, first trip on an airplane. Talk about the "voice" that students give the character in the entry. Is there a way the journal entry can be written to make it sound like the voice of the character in the video?

After-Viewing Activity

Keep video journals. After seeing a video, but before the class discusses anything, ask students to make entries in their journals. Suggest that each student's entry be "written" by one of the characters in the video. Thus, each will need to think about the character's "voice."

PURPOSE: TO ENJOY WORDS AND BUILD VOCABULARY

Videos offer an opportunity to pique children's curiosity about words and to let them hear other people speaking and enjoying words—their sounds, their meanings, their occasional silliness, and the joy of finding just the right word to make a point. Seek out videos that dramatize the work of master wordsmiths such as Rudyard Kipling and share with your class the writers' powerful use of words.

Grades: K–3

Suggested Title: *The Elephant's Child*

Grades: 4–6

Suggested Titles: *How the Leopard Got His Spots; How the Camel Got His Hump/How the Rhinoceros Got His Skin* (available in several adaptations; select the one you think has the best narration)

Before-Viewing Activity

Look through the stories in Kipling's *The Jungle Book* and note several of the unusual words, such as *bulgy, satiable curiosity, O Best Beloved,* and *Bi-Coloured-Python-Rock-Snake*. Ask if anyone knows any of the meanings. Suggest that students listen for these words as you read the stories to them. Encourage them to close their eyes and visualize the action. Talk about the words; delight in them! What other words do the children like? List them. Ask again if anyone knows any of the meanings after they have heard them used within the context of a story.

After-Viewing Activities
- Invite younger children to draw pictures of the words. For older groups, suggest that they include these new words in stories and their own speech.
- Keep a running list of new and terrific words learned in videos.
- Younger children will enjoy acting out the different animals the elephant encounters on his journey.
- For younger children who still may not be able to distinguish between what is real and what is pretend, invite each child in the class to make a paper-bag mask of a favorite imaginary character seen in a video or book. Encourage them to pretend to be the characters they choose.
- Ask the class what clues are given in the video to help viewers identify the region where the story takes place.

PURPOSE: TO EXPLORE THE CONCEPT OF EVIL IN CHARACTERS

Grades: K–6

Suggested Titles: *Oliver!; Treasure Island*

Additional Titles To Consider: *Adventures of Huckleberry Finn; Merlin and the Dragons; The Wizard of Oz*

Before-Viewing Discussion
Discuss with students evil characters. What does *evil* mean? Why is someone evil? If a character is evil, is there one or more reasons he or she is that way? See if you can break down the evil in a person to learn what caused it.

From *Merlin and the Dragons*. Photo courtesy of Lightyear Entertainment, L.P.

PURPOSE: TO UNDERSTAND HEROES/HEROINES

Grades: K–3

Suggested Titles: *Thumbelina*; "The Little Dragon" (told by Jay O'Callahan on *Family Circle Presents Storyland Theatre*, Vol. 1)

Additional Titles To Consider: *The Cricket in Times Square; The Wind in the Willows;* "The Wizard" (in *The Mysterious Tadpole and Other Stories*)

After-Viewing Activity

Children love small heroes and animals in literature because they readily identify with the characters. After

96 Connecting Activities with Specific Videos

showing a video fairy tale or animal story, invite a group of children to act out the story. Some quick and easy costumes are useful to spur on the imagination and are fun for children to make.

PURPOSE: TO EXPLORE THE CONCEPT OF GOING ON A QUEST AND HOW IT RELATES TO PLOT AND CHARACTER DEVELOPMENT

Grades: K–3

Suggested Titles: *The Hobbit*; "The Story about Ping" (in *The Story about Ping and Other Stories*); "Where the Wild Things Are" (in *The Maurice Sendak Library*)

Additional Titles To Consider: *Babar the Little Elephant; The Elephant's Child*

Before-Viewing Discussion

Discuss what a quest is. Identify videos in which a character goes on a journey and returns wiser. What other stories would fit this category? Would "Harold and the Purple Crayon" (in *Scholastic Blue Ribbon Storybook Video*, Vol. 2) or "Panama" (in *Corduroy and Other Bear Stories*) be considered quest stories? Are quest stories always centered on a boy or man?

Grades: 4–6

Suggested Titles: *The Adventures of Milo and Otis; The Land of Faraway; The Adventures of Robin Hood; Walking on Air*

Before- and After-Viewing Discussions

What is the purpose of stories describing a character's quest? The ones cited above take place in the past or future, not the present. Is this always the case? Ask your students if they have ever been on a quest. Can they create a quest story, complete with characters, of their own?

What else can be learned about quest stories? Can students remember stories they read when they were younger that would be considered quest stories?

After-Viewing Activity

Have students select a quest story and build a diorama of it. The diorama should focus on the climax of the story, when the character achieves his or her desired quest.

Exploring and Understanding How Videos Portray and Evoke Emotions

Grades: K–6

Suggested Titles: *Ashpet: An American Cinderella*; "Corduroy" (in *Corduroy and Other Bear Stories*; *A Link with Nature*; "Where the Wild Things Are" (in *The Maurice Sendak Library*)

Additional Titles To Consider: Ramona Series; *The Diary of Anne Frank*; *Never Cry Wolf*; *Sarah and the Squirrel*

Before-Viewing Discussion

Ask students to suggest different emotions, such as love, hate, fear, anger, sadness, frustration, and stubbornness, and list them on the chalkboard. Discuss and list tapes that show emotion, beginning with tapes for young children and working up to tapes appropriate for your class.

After-Viewing Activity

Divide the class into groups and ask them to isolate segments within tapes that demonstrate specific emotions. Ask each group to share three of their findings. The children will need to (1) identify the emotion, (2) locate a segment in a tape demonstrating the emotion, and (3) cue up the tape at the segment in order to show it to the class.

Using Video To Explore How Others Live

Grades: K–6

Suggested Title: *Molly's Pilgrim*

Additional Titles To Consider: *Cricket's Clubhouse: Around the World with Cricket; Discover Korea; Gift of the Whales; I'd Like To Teach the World To Sing*

The story of *Molly's Pilgrim* appeals to people of all ages, from children as young as 5 or 6 to adults. Younger children tend to comment on specific incidents from the story (Arthur and the pencil, Molly and gymnastics), while children in second and third grades want to know if it is a true story and ask how Molly got out of Russia.

Children in the middle years focus on the characters and how they all interact. Because the children in the video are in about third grade, older children may wonder why you are showing them something that they think is too young for them. Explain that although the characters are younger than they, the story's theme speaks to all ages. Once the tape has begun, no one will question why you are showing it—they will all be too involved. This video ties in with many themes, including Thanksgiving, the immigrant experience, Russia, Judaism, belonging, and being ostracized.

Molly's Pilgrim needs some preliminary explanation. You may want to read Barbara Cohen's book (published by Lothrop, Lee & Shepard) to the class before showing the video, as well as hold a class discussion to learn what prior knowledge students have about Russia.

Grades: K–3

Before-Viewing Discussion

Ask children to name different feelings. List them.

After-Viewing Activity

Ask children to divide a piece of paper into four equal

parts and draw four different feelings that were evoked while watching the video. As the students draw, note their conversations with each other for later discussion.

Grades: 4–6

Before-Viewing Discussion

Ask children to think about all of the different feelings that exist. List them on the chalkboard. Have each student draw a "here-and-now wheel" on a piece of paper (see Glossary). At significant moments during the video, ask them to note their feelings on spokes of their wheels. After the video, discuss the specific segments and ask for volunteers to share their notations. It might be useful to note the VCR counter numbers so you can fast forward to the segments for review.

Using Video To Understand Communication

PURPOSE: TO UNDERSTAND OTHER FORMS OF COMMUNICATION

Grades: K–3

Suggested Title: *Sign Me a Story* (choose either "Little Red Riding Hood" or "Goldilocks and the Three Bears")

Before-Viewing Discussion

Discuss what the word *communicate* means. What is the purpose of communication? How do people communicate with each other? Are humans the only animals who communicate? How do people who cannot hear communicate with others?

After-Viewing Discussion

Ask for volunteers to use sign language to tell a story. What else can be learned about sign language?

Grades: 4–6

Suggested Titles: *Say It by Signing; Sign Me a Story* (choose either "Little Red Riding Hood" or "Goldilocks and the Three Bears")

Before-Viewing Discussion

Discuss what the word *communicate* means. What is the purpose of communication? How do people communicate with each other? Are humans the only animals who communicate? How do people who cannot hear communicate with others? Have you ever tried to tell someone something but you felt they were not listening? Sometimes people talk at the same time. Note when this happens on TV and how characters deal with it. What would have been a better approach to communicating?

After-Viewing Activity

Ask for volunteers to use sign language to tell a story. What else can be learned about sign language?

PURPOSE: TO LEARN ABOUT CLOSED CAPTIONS

Grades: K–6

Suggested Titles: any title with closed captions (These titles can be identified by the letters CC, for closed captioned, or by the National Captioning Institute's trademark. This one company captions more than 90 percent of videos with closed captions. The company's logo is a cube with a tail coming out of the bottom. Many Disney titles, Random House's "Sesame Street" titles, and Playhouse Video titles have closed captions.)

Before-Viewing Discussion

Closed captions offer nonhearing people an entry to television. With a closed-caption decoder, dialogue appears in subtitles at the bottom of the screen. These subtitles are much like those seen in foreign films. The decoder

Above: Still from "Sesame Street" as viewed through closed-caption decoder. Photo courtesy of the National Captioning Institute.

Left: Official trademark of the National Captioning Institute.

has other uses, too. Discuss ways to use this piece of technology to help people who are learning English as a second language.

Before-Viewing Activity

The decoder is also useful for encouraging people to read. Attempt to borrow a decoder and locate a video with closed captions. Watch the program together with students, noting any mistakes in spelling and syntax. Now find a program on television with closed captions and watch it together, again noting any spelling mistakes or problems of syntax.

Ask for a volunteer or volunteers to research more about closed captions and report back to the class. How is it done? When a television show is live, what happens to the captions? (See Appendix B for the address of the National Captioning Institute.)

Using Video To Teach Critical Viewing

PURPOSE: TO UNDERSTAND
THE POWER OF THE MESSAGE

Grades: 4–6

Suggested Title: *Buy Me That!*

Before-Viewing Activity

Ask students to list the ways that video, film, and TV influence or change people's points of view on topics such as the importance of clothes in people's lives, morality, and war. The discussion might include thoughts concerning television coverage of the daily news and the impact of commercials on people's buying decisions.

Grades: K–6

Support Activity

Ask children to list the television shows and videos they have seen in the past week. Encourage them to look for patterns in their viewing habits. Is their viewing menu balanced, with nonfiction and fiction, animated and live-action shows? How much TV and video are they watching each day? What other activities do they enjoy? What do they do while they are watching TV or video?

How much do they remember about a program watched last week? What did they learn from it? Was it a good way to spend time? Why or why not? What else might they ask about a TV show?

Learning To Evaluate Videos and Television

Grades: 4–6

Suggested Titles: *Beauty and the Beast* (the Hi-Tops adaptation); *What's a Good Story? Beauty and the Beast*

After-Viewing Activity

Discuss with the children the elements of the story of "Beauty and the Beast," including plot, which includes characters and some form of conflict; setting; and theme, the overall message of the story. How does this production fare?

Now watch *What's a Good Story? Beauty and the Beast.* Discuss the points made in this straightforward and clear explanation about the elements that are necessary for a good story.

Using Video To Practice Creating and Using an Outline

Grades: 5–6

Watch *What's a Good Story? Beauty and the Beast* again.

After-Viewing Activity

Create with the students on the chalkboard an outline of the important points as they are discussed on the video. As a class, agree on an outline form and duplicate it for

104 Connecting Activities with Specific Videos

From *What's a Good Story? Beauty and the Beast.* Photo courtesy of Lightyear Entertainment, L.P.

each child (leave plenty of space throughout the outline for children to be able to fill in comments later on). The children will use this outline to judge prime-time television.

Assign children to watch a half-hour situation comedy on television. While watching, each child should take careful notes that will enable him or her to participate in a class discussion in school the next day. Compare and contrast the quality of the two stories: "Beauty and the Beast" and the sitcom. What can be learned?

Now that the outline has been prepared, give it a snappy title and assign it often. This is a useful exercise to help students evaluate the quality of all programming. What stands up to this scrutiny and what does not?

Using Video for Research

PURPOSE: TO ENCOURAGE STUDENTS TO USE VIDEO AS AN ADDITIONAL SOURCE OF INFORMATION FOR RESEARCH PROJECTS

Grades: K–3

Suggested Titles: *Animal Alphabet; Animals of Africa; Animal Zoop* (Vol. 2)

>Additional Titles To Consider: any in the VideoTours Great America series or Science/Nature Collection; *Where in the World: Kids Explore Kenya*

Before-Viewing Discussion

Each child selects an animal he or she would like to learn more about and researches that animal. As part of the report, each child locates video footage documenting the selected animal (see Appendix A for suggestions).

Demonstrate to the children how to cue up a tape (see Glossary) and how to use the VCR's counter to find specific footage.

If your class has a regularly scheduled library period, discuss the project with the librarian and ask to have animal books shown to the class. From these resource books, each student selects an animal to learn more about. Students should learn some of the following facts about their selected animals: size, color, habitat, food, movement, behavior, and any other interesting facts. Videos in the *Animal Zoop* series answer these questions, and they are well suited to children in the early primary years.

This activity can be done with children in kindergarten through sixth grade. The expectations will obviously change as children get older, but all children can use animal books to locate animals that they want to learn more about.

Grades: 4–6

Suggested Titles: *Animals of Africa; Animal Wonders from Down Under; Monterey Bay Aquarium; A World Alive*

Discussion Activity

Show the class a video with unusual animals and ask each student to select an animal to research. In addition to written reports, each student must locate a three-minute segment of video footage that features the selected animal to share with the class. Encourage students to locate a superb short segment rather than a longer but mediocre one.

Support Activity

Demonstrate how to cue up a tape and how to use the VCR's counter to find specific footage.

From *A World Alive*. Photo courtesy of Sea Studios.

SEVEN

Helping Parents Cope with Video

Adults who work with children and media need to be conscious of how children perceive video images and how their understanding of these images changes as they get older. Parents also need to appreciate the power of the media and to regulate their children's exposure to inappropriate images and story lines.

Perhaps the best way for educators to help parents cope with the onslaught of media in their children's lives is to help them understand how differently the same image is perceived by children of different ages. When children listen to a story such as "The Three Little Pigs," they "produce" the pictures in their own minds, creating images with which they feel comfortable; for example, a wolf that is not too menacing— maybe a little furry creature that resembles a cat, or, if they are feeling brave, a wolf with teeth, maybe even sharp teeth. The point is that the children themselves create the characters, rather than a filmmaker or a book illustrator.

When children look at a picture book showing an illustrator's rendition of a story, they still have some control over their relationship with scary images such as the wolf. They can cover the picture with a hand, turn the page, or even close the book. But to very young children watching a video of the same story, the wolf on the screen is able to jump out of the screen and gobble them up. Preschoolers have a different sense from older children and adults of what is real and what is pretend. From preschoolers' point of view, that wolf in the TV is real, just as real as "Mister Rogers' Neighborhood," which, of course, from their point of view, exists in the television.

Compare the experiences of three children watching a live-action alphabet video—a 17-month-old toddler, a preschooler, and a second or third grader. On the screen, the toddler sees a blue sky and a swamp with some trees hanging over it. Some bugs are flying around, and there is a lovely flock of soaring birds. Slithering about in the water is a long colorful creature. The toddler exclaims and points to the creature's teeth. Perhaps she is able to identify them as teeth and points to her own. Upbeat music encourages her to sway and she claps her hands. Her older brother, age 3 or 4, identifies the creature slithering in the sunshine as an alligator. Yikes! More sophisticated in the ways of the world, he knows that alligators have sharp teeth and that they are ferocious. He also "knows" that the alligator can crawl right into the room and gobble them both up. The oldest child watching the video recognizes that the alligator stands for *A*. He has a firmer grasp of real and pretend than do the younger children, and knows that they are watching a video and that the alligator cannot exit from the screen into the room to devour him. After he identifies the alligator, his mind may skip ahead as he wonders what animal will be shown for the letter *K* or *T* or *U*.

While the toddler sees the alligator's movement and color and is drawn to the music, the preschooler knows that the alligator is dangerous. The second grader probably has amassed considerable factual information about alligators, as well as other animals, and he begins to speculate about what animals will represent specific letters of the alphabet. Three children see the same image, yet each has a different response to it.

Thus, children of different ages bring very different knowledge and understanding of life in general to the video experience. The same thing happens, of course, with reading—children of different ages have different reactions to the same images. However, viewers do not have the same control over an image on a screen as they do when listening to a story or reading a book.

Regulating Children's Video Consumption

Although too many children waste their time and minds by watching violent or mindless videos, alternatives do exist, along with ways for parents to determine a tape's content before placing it in a VCR. It is possible for parents to allow their children to watch videos without harming them. Teachers and media specialists can help parents by providing them with tools for tape selection. I recommend that parents take the following steps:

1. Search out video reviews written by people with knowledge of both child development and video. Two sources are local newspapers and parenting magazines. Many large towns and cities publish parenting magazines, and many of these include video columns that review both new releases and older tapes. Video stores often offer a review source for worthwhile new releases. Librarians and classroom teachers can also compile and distribute annotated lists of titles that have been recommended.

2. When looking at a video in the store or library, scrutinize the box, noting the artwork. The illustrations or photographs used on the cover will generally reflect the best the tape has to offer. If the photograph is dark, the footage on the inside of the tape probably is, too. By reading the small print on the box, parents will learn what the producer and distributor want people to know about the tape's contents. Are age suggestions given? Is the tape an adaptation of a book, or is it rehashed Saturday morning cartoons focusing on a licensed toy character? Has the tape won any awards? Aside from Emmys, Oscars, and Grammys, look for CINE Golden

Eagle, Action for Children's Television, and Film Advisory Board awards. Film and/or video awards are given by the American Film and Video Festival, National Educational Film & Video Festival, Parents' Choice, ViRA (*Video Review* magazine), and American Video Conference.

3. While looking in a library or video store for a video to watch at home, use other parents as a resource for learning about tapes. Ask other browsing parents if they are familiar with particular tapes. If they are, ask them questions such as the following: What is it about? Is it scary or violent? Is it good entertainment, or a waste of my child's time and my money? Other worthwhile sources of information are librarians and video store clerks. If you cannot find anyone who knows about a tape, pass on it for the time being. If it is good, it will eventually turn up in reviews or on lists of award-winning titles. If it is just another entry in the "mindless media" category of children's programming, parents can reward themselves for having been discriminating consumers.

The Value of Children's Video

Many videos that appeal to children will not necessarily be enjoyed by adults. Tapes that seem insipid or boring by adult standards may have value for children. The important issue to consider is what a child will take away from the viewing experience. Is the tape satisfying emotional needs? Are new songs being learned? Is the viewer seeing something he or she would not see otherwise? Are children in the tape having genuine fun? Laughing at silly jokes? For entertainment and in controlled doses, such tapes are fine.

It is also true that children often have to learn to appreciate what adults consider to be the best in children's programming. *The Velveteen Rabbit*, *The Steadfast Tin Soldier*, and *Pecos Bill* are three videos from a series produced by

Rabbit Ears Productions and distributed by Random House and SVS, Inc. These tapes have won many awards, but they may not be adored or appreciated by a child on first viewing. Suggest to parents that they watch one of these with their child and engage in a conversation discussing one or two of its merits (they should not overdo this). With time and further film criticism discussions, children will learn to appreciate a tape's qualities. Remind parents that it took them 20-some-odd years to develop a sense of humor and to cultivate tastes in food, literature, film, and the finer things in life. A child's tastes are still developing. For the moment, Mister Rogers' neighborhood may be the place a child most wants to be.

Children's abilities to deal with stories, images, and sound effects change as they grow, along with their interpretations of and responses to particular videos. Dumbo's separation from his mother probably does not disturb a 2-year-old, who focuses on the images and the music, rather than the story, but it may be upsetting to a 4-year-old, who knows that if he were separated from his mother he would be sad, too. A 7- or 8-year-old sees this scene as poignant, but knows that it is an animated story (or cartoon, depending on what the child calls this art form) about an animal who is very different from her.

Fairy tales with clear and easy-to-understand morals are among the stories most requested by children, for good reason. They provide the backdrop for myriad visual delights—princes, castles, fairy godmothers, talking toads—all cleverly produced within young heads. With the help of scriptwriters such as the Brothers Grimm, Hans Christian Andersen, and Charles Perrault, heroes and villains encounter a multitude of adventures in which the former live happily ever after and the latter receive their just desserts.

Children benefit from fairy tales in many ways. Problematic plots stimulate their imaginations and present models for daydreams, arousing curiosity, clarifying emotions, and offering comfort through stories with which they can identify. The moralistic tales are straightforward—human beings, witches, goblins, ogres, and anthropomorphic animals embody either good or evil, rarely anything in between. Fairy tales can be reassuring to young children. Presented with people who are "ever so very good" in print, on the screen, or in real life, they may think, "I'm not that good. What's wrong with me? Am I an awful person?" By hearing stories with characters who are good and bad, children can work through their less-than-nice thoughts and learn that they are not alone.

When children first hear fairy tales, they create pictures in their minds of such scenes as Gretel pushing the wicked witch into the oven, the house where the seven dwarfs lived, and the big bad wolf's dazzling teeth. When children are introduced to illustrated books and Technicolor tapes after they have heard the tales and made them their own, they bring their existing understanding of the tales, complete with pictures of how the stories "look." Their powers of imagination are then further stimulated by incorporating what they like in the videos into what they have already imagined.

Only after a child has heard a fairy tale several times and feels comfortable with it, knowing that the good emerge victorious, should he or she be introduced to the story in books or on the screen. Beautiful illustrations or animation, or live action with glorious scenery and perhaps a dash of special effects, enhances the familiar stories. Right before children's eyes, heroes struggle to overcome trials with hard work, help from others, magic, or time acting in their favor.

Fairy tales fulfill some of the important criteria used in selecting a tape for home viewing. In addition to the familiarity that they enjoy among children, they are the most classic of stories.

Deciding Which Tape To Choose

With nursery rhymes, Raffi's music, and *BabySongs* (Hi-Tops) under their belts, preschoolers are ready for stories with a beginning, middle, and end. Implicit in the notion of a story is conflict between the hero or heroine and a clearly defined villain. Many 3-year-olds have love/hate relationships with these scary villains; on one level the children are frightened by them, but on another they are curious and want more. With each successful encounter they achieve an enormous sense of accomplishment. As they "shake hands" with the villain, they are able to feel victorious.

When selecting a tape of a fairy tale or other story, the key issues to consider are what the story is about, how the characters are presented, and how the villain is depicted. As an example of the ways productions can vary, consider four adaptations of "The Three Little Pigs." A parent or teacher choosing one of these tapes will need to look at how the production presents the pigs and the "big bad wolf." Do the pigs' voices tell anything about their personalities? Does the wolf look menacingly real, with his teeth accentuated?

In selecting a tape for a 3-year-old, parents should keep in mind where the child is in relation to "monsters." The villain should not be too scary. A good version of "The Three Little Pigs" for children this age is on *Three Richard Scarry Animal Nursery Tales* (Golden Book), which offers a straightforward presentation with only the bare bones of the story. When the wolf is first introduced, words are shown on the screen as the narrator sings "big bad wolf." (The mere mention of the word *wolf* is enough to set off squeals!) This gives the child time to think about and prepare for the wolf. Further into the story a fairly benign wolf is shown, true to Richard Scarry's style.

Another version of "The Three Little Pigs" (in *Three Billy Goats Gruff/The Three Little Pigs*, SVS) includes more details of the story along with a realistic wolf, complete with sharp teeth and talon-like claws. The story is rich with humor and will appeal to 4- and 5-year-olds, as well as their older siblings. Narrator Holly Hunter creates colorful voices for each of the characters, and Art Lande's music sets the tone. The pigs are females, adding a twist to the story that will be noted by parents but probably won't mean much to children. David Jorgensen's soft-hued illustrations may appeal more to parents than to their offspring (offering another opportunity to refine children's appreciation for the finer things in life), but because of Hunter's stellar narration and children's love for the story, this adaptation works.

The version that requires the most courage and that is the most sophisticated and demanding of the viewer is included in *Happy Birthday, Moon and Other Stories* (CC Studios), adapted from Erik Blevgvad's retelling of the story. Children ages 5 and 6 are up to the challenge of this version, and will appreciate the depth of characterization. They have a clearer understanding of real versus pretend and are better armed to tackle the scarier images found in this version than are younger children. The wonderfully threatening wolf is fully appreciated by kindergarten audiences. Viewers enjoy the fun as the wolf huffs and puffs and blows in the pigs' ill-made houses. This is a detailed adaptation, with more embellishments than the versions described above.

Faerie Tale Theatre's *The Three Little Pigs* (Playhouse) uses live action, with well-known performers (Billy Crystal, Jeff Goldblum, Valerie Perrine in a newly scripted part, and Fred Willard) playing the parts of pigs and the big-bad-very-evil wolf. This novel production relies heavily on humor and sarcasm, which appeals to many children 6 and older.

Many wonderful tapes are available for parents to share with their children. Teachers and media specialists can help parents with suggestions and guidance, as well as by working in the classroom to teach children to be discerning viewers. Television and video have the potential to be both harmful and beneficial. By teaching children to be television and video critics, and by offering them the best programming available, educators can challenge and nurture young minds, and offer children valuable information that will enhance their lives both now and in the future.

APPENDIX A

Suggested Video Titles

This section presents a list of videos recommended for children followed by a subject/genre category index of the same titles. All of these titles were available as of January 1991. Videos in the first list are arranged alphabetically by title, and each is followed by the name of the producer/distributor, suggested age groups, video producers' series if applicable, and categories. (The age groups given are meant as guidelines, not as hard-and-fast rules.) Individual titles are listed for series, and individual story segments are also listed for most anthologies.

If a video falls into more than one category, every appropriate category is listed. Categories used include:

  Adaptation Fairy Tales Language Arts
  Animals   & Legends Multiculture
  Animation Family   Music
  Biography Fantasy (8 & Up) Reference
  Coming of Age Fine Arts   Science
  Environment History   Travel

Video series for children:

  Children's Circle/CC Studios
  From the Brothers Grimm
  Rabbit Ears Productions
  Reading Rainbow
  Stories To Remember
  WonderWorks

Suggested Video Titles

NOTE: Because videos often have short licensing agreements, distributors for some videos in this list may have changed since this volume went to press. For example, *What's Happening to Me?* used to be an LCA title, but it is now carried by Starmaker.

Alphabetical List

Abe Lincoln: Freedom Fighter
VidAmerica
Ages 6–12
    Biography, History

Abel's Island
Random House
Ages 6–12
    Adaptation, Animals, Animation, Language Arts

The Adventures of Huckleberry Finn
MGM/UA
Ages 5 and up
    Adaptation, Coming of Age, History, Language Arts, Multiculture

The Adventures of Milo and Otis
RCA/Columbia
All ages
    Animals, Travel

The Adventures of Robin Hood
MGM/UA
Ages 6 and up
    Adaptation, History

Alice in Wonderland
Disney
Ages 4–8
    Adaptation, Animation, Language Arts, Music

Amahl and the Night Visitors (opera)
Video Artists International
Ages 6 and up
    Adaptation, Fine Arts, History, Language Arts, Multiculture, Music

The Amazing Bone and Other Stories
Includes "John Brown and the Midnight Cat," "A Picture for Harold's Room," "The Trip"
CC Studios
Series: Children's Circle
Ages 3–8
    Adaptation, Animation, Language Arts

AMERICAN STORYTELLING STORIES
(8 titles)
H. W. Wilson
Ages 6 and up
    Adaptation, Fairy Tales & Legends, Language Arts, Reference

An American Tail
MCA
Ages 6–8
    Animals, Animation, History, Multiculture

And the Children Shall Lead
Public Media Video
Series: WonderWorks
Ages 6–12
    History, Multiculture

Animal ABCs
Creative Video Concepts
Ages 6 and under
    Animals, Environment,
    Language Arts, Reference,
    Science

ANIMAL ALPHABET (3 titles)
Series includes *Animal Alphabet, Animal Babies in the Wild; Baby Animals Just Want To Have Fun*
Warner
Ages 8 and under
    Animals, Language Arts,
    Music

Animal Stories
Includes "Petunia," "Why Mosquitoes Buzz in People's Ears," "Andy and the Lion"
CC Studios
Series: Children's Circle
Ages 3–8
    Adaptation, Animation,
    Language Arts

Animal Talk
Family Express
Ages 5–11
    Adaptation, Animals

ANIMAL WONDERS FROM DOWN UNDER (7 titles)
Series includes *Crocodiles/Reptiles; Fauna of Australia; The Little Marsupials/The Kangaroos; Platypus/The Islands; The Remarkable Bandicoots/World of Koala; Silver Gulls/Mallee Fowl; The Tiny Carnivores/Wombat*
Pacific Arts
Ages 7–12
    Animals, Environment,
    Reference, Science, Travel

ANIMAL ZOOP, VOL. 2 (10 titles)
Series includes *Camels; Cheetahs; Gazelles; Gibbons; Hippopotamuses; Lions; Marmosets and Tamarins; Penguins; Rhinoceroses; Water Animals of the Cascade*
Creative Video Concepts
Ages 5 and up
    Animals, Environment,
    Reference, Science

ANIMALS IN ACTION (12 titles)
Series includes *Animals of the Night; Baby Birds; Desert Animals and Plants; Fresh Water Animals; Frogs and Toads; How Animals Move; How Animals Talk; Mountain Animals; Record-breaking Animals; Spiders; Tree Living Animals; The Turtle Family*
Kodak
Ages 7–12
    Animals, Environment,
    Reference, Science

Animals of Africa
Concord
Ages 5–12
    Animals, Reference, Travel

Animated Haggadah
Ergo Media
Ages 6–12
    Animation, History,
    Multiculture, Reference

Anne of Avonlea
Disney
Series: WonderWorks
Ages 6 and up
    Adaptation, Family

Anne of Green Gables
Disney
Series: WonderWorks
Ages 6 and up
    Adaptation, Family

ARMCHAIR SAFARIS (2 titles)
Series includes *Masai Mara Lions/Virunga Gorillas; Serengeti Migration/Amboseli Elephants*
EcoVentures
Ages 8 and up
    Animals, Environment, Reference, Travel

Arthur's Eyes
Vestron
Series: Reading Rainbow
Ages 4–9
    Adaptation, Multiculture

As the Wind Rocks the Wagon
APL Educational Video
Ages 10 and up
    Biography, History, Reference

Ashpet: An American Cinderella
Davenport Films
Series: From the Brothers Grimm
Ages 5 and up
    Adaptation, Fairy Tales & Legends, Language Arts, Multiculture

THE AUTHOR'S EYE (2 titles)
Series includes *Roald Dahl* (ages 8–12), *Katherine Paterson* (ages 10–14)
Random House
    Biography, Language Arts, Reference

The Autobiography of Miss Jane Pittman
Prism
Ages 7 and up
    Adaptation, History, Language Arts, Multiculture

BABAR (5 titles)
Babar and Father Christmas
Hi-Tops
Ages 4–8
    Adaptation, Animals, Animation, Language Arts

Babar et le Pere Noel
Gessler
Ages 3 and up
    Adaptation, Animals, Animation, Family, Language Arts

Babar the Elephant Comes to America
Vestron
Ages 4–8
    Adaptation, Animals, Animation, Family, Language Arts

Babar the Little Elephant
Vestron
Ages 4–8
    Adaptation, Animals, Animation, Family Language Arts

Babar the Movie
Family Home Entertainment
Ages 5–8
    Adaptation, Animals, Animation, Family, Language Arts

Baboons, Butterflies and Me
The Nature Company
Ages 7 and under
    Animals, Music

Bach and Broccoli
Family Home Entertainment
Ages 7 and up
    Family

Ballet for Beginners
Kultur
Ages 5 and up
    Fine Arts, Music

Banana, Banana, Banana Slug
Bullfrog Films
Ages 4–9
    Animals, Environment, Language Arts, Science

BANK STREET READ-ALONG STORY VIDEOS (5 titles)
Series includes *A Dozen Dizzy Dogs; Follow That Fish; Mr. Bubble Gum; Mr. Monster; Not Now! Said the Cow*
Best Film & Video
Ages 6 and under
    Adaptation, Animation, Language Arts

Barney and the Backyard Gang: Barney Goes to School
Lyons Group
Ages 3–8
    Language Arts, Music

BBC Language Course: Muzzy French
Addison-Wesley
Ages 5–10
    Animation, Multiculture, Reference

BBC Language Course: Muzzy Spanish
Addison-Wesley
Ages 5–10
    Animation, Multiculture, Reference

Be a Juggler
Mid-Com
Ages 8 and up
    Reference

Be a Magician
Mid-Com
Ages 6 and up
    Reference

Beauty and the Beast
Hi-Tops
Series: Stories To Remember
Ages 5–9
    Adaptation, Animation, Coming of Age, Language Arts

Beauty and the Beast
Nelson
Ages 10 and up
    Adaptation, Coming of Age, Language Arts

Big Bird in China
Random House
Ages 4–8
    Language Arts, Multiculture, Travel

The Black Stallion
MGM/UA
Ages 8 and up
    Adaptation, Animals, Travel

The Black Stallion Returns
MGM/UA
Ages 8 and up
    Adaptation, Animals, Travel

THE BLUE FRONTIER (13 titles)
Series includes *Antarctic Adventure; Aquaspace Adventure; Clown or Criminal; Gigi's Legacy; King of the Sea; Nature's Playground; The Rescuers; Sea of Many Moods; Shark Shark Shark; Tales from the Nursery; To Save a Whale; Underseas Eden; Vanishing Mermaids*
Bennett Marine Video
Ages 10 and up
    Animals, Environment, Science, Travel

Booker
Disney
Series: WonderWorks
Ages 7–12
    Biography, History, Multiculture

Born Free
RCA/Columbia
Ages 6 and up
    Adaptation, Animals, Travel

Suggested Video Titles

The Box of Delights
Simon & Schuster
Series: WonderWorks
Ages 8–12
    Adaptation, Language Arts

The Boy Who Could Fly
Lorimar
Ages 8–12
    Coming of Age, Family, Fantasy (8 & Up)

The Bridge to Terabithia
Public Media Video
Series: Wonderworks
Ages 7–14
    Adaptation, Family, Language Arts

The Brothers Lionheart
Pacific Arts
Ages 8–14
    Adaptation, Fantasy (8 & Up)

Bugs and Daffy's Carnival of the Animals
Warner
Ages 5 and up
    Animals, Animation, Music

Buster's World
Specialty Video
Series: WonderWorks
Ages 8 and up
    Family, Fantasy (8 & Up), Language Arts

Buy Me That!
Films, Inc.
Ages 7–14
    Reference

Captains Courageous
MGM/UA
Ages 7 and up
    Adaptation, History, Language Arts

Carnival of the Animals
Twin Tower
Ages 4–10
    Animals, Fine Arts, Music

Carnival of the Animals
Video Artists International
Ages 8 and up
    Fine Arts, Music

Castle
PBS Video
Ages 8 and up
    Adaptation, Animation, Fine Arts, History, Language Arts, Reference

Cathedral
PBS Video
Ages 8 and up
    Adaptation, Animation, Fine Arts, History, Language Arts, Reference

Chanuka at Bubbe's
Classic Telepublishing
Ages 5–12
    Multiculture, Music, Reference

CHARLIE CHAPLIN (5 titles)
Series includes *The Chaplin Revue; The Circus/A Day's Pleasure; City Lights; The Kid/The Idle Class; The Gold Rush/Pay Day*
Playhouse
Ages 7 and up
    Language Arts

Charlotte's Web
Paramount
Ages 6–8
    Adaptation, Animals, Animation, Language Arts, Music

The Children of Theatre Street
Kultur
Ages 7 and up

Alphabetical List 121

Fine Arts, Multiculture, Music, Travel

A Child's Christmas in Wales
Vestron
Ages 5 and up
Adaptation, Family, Multiculture, Travel

Chitty Chitty Bang Bang
MGM/UA
Ages 5 and up
Adaptation

Choosing the Best in Children's Video
ALA
Adults
Reference

A Christmas Carol
Crocus Entertainment
Family (6 and up)
Adaptation, Family, Fine Arts, Language Arts

Christmas Stories
Includes "Morris' Disappearing Bag," "The Clown of God," "The Little Drummer Boy," "The Twelve Days of Christmas"
CC Studios
Series: Children's Circle
Ages 3–8
Adaptation, Animation, Language Arts

Cinderella: Rodgers and Hammerstein
Playhouse
All ages
Adaptation, Music

Classic Fairy Tales
Includes "The Ugly Duckling," "The Emperor's New Clothes," "The Princess and the Pea," "Rapunzel," "The Four Musicians," "Puss in Boots"
Family Home Entertainment
Ages 4–8
Adaptation, Animation, Fairy Tales & Legends

Clifford's Fun (6 titles)
Series includes *Clifford's Fun with Letters*; *Clifford's Fun with Numbers*; *Clifford's Fun with Opposites*; *Clifford's Fun with Rhymes*; *Clifford's Fun with Shapes*; *Clifford's Fun with Sounds*
Family Home Entertainment
Ages 3–7
Adaptation, Animation

A Connecticut Yankee at King Arthur's Court
MCA
Ages 7 and up
Adaptation, History, Language Arts

Corduroy and Other Bear Stories
Also includes "Panama," "Blueberries for Sal"
CC Studios
Series: Children's Circle
Ages 3–10
Adaptation, Animation/Live Action, Language Arts

THE CRICKET IN TIMES SQUARE (3 titles)
Family Home Entertainment
Ages 4–8
Adaptation, Animals, Animation, Language Arts

Cricket's Clubhouse: Around the World with Cricket
Hi-Tops
Age 4–8
Animation, Travel

122 Suggested Video Titles

Dark Crystal
HBO
Ages 6 and up
    Animation

David Copperfield
MGM/UA
Ages 7 and up
    Adaptation, Coming of Age, History, Language Arts

The Devil and Daniel Mouse
Warner
Ages 4–10
    Adaptation, Animals, Animation

The Diary of Anne Frank
CBS/Fox
Ages 10 and up
    Adaptation, Biography, History, Multiculture

Digging Up Dinosaurs
Vestron
Series: Reading Rainbow
Ages 5–10
    Adaptation, Animals, Science

Dinosaur!
Vestron
Ages 5–12
    Animals, Science

Dinosaurs!
Golden Book
Ages 4–12
    Animals, Animation, Science

Discover Korea
Asia Society
Ages 9 and up
    Multiculture, Travel

Doctor De Soto and Other Stories
Also includes "Patrick," "Curious George Rides a Bike," "The Hat"
CC Studios
Series: Children's Circle
Ages 3–8
    Adaptation, Animals, Animation, Language Arts

Don't Eat the Pictures
Random House
Ages 4–8
    Fine Arts

DR. SEUSS (12 titles):
ABC
Random House
Ages 2–6
    Adaptation, Language Arts
The Butter Battle Book
Kids Klassics
Ages 5 and up
    Animation, Environment, Science
The Cat in the Hat
Playhouse
Ages 2–6
    Adaptation, Animation, Language Arts
The Cat in the Hat Comes Back
Random House
Ages 2–6
    Adaptation, Animation, Language Arts
Dr. Seuss Festival
MGM/UA
Ages 2–6
    Adaptation, Animation, Language Arts
Dr. Seuss on the Loose
Playhouse
Ages 2–6
    Adaptation, Animation, Language Arts
The Grinch Grinches Cat in the Hat/ Pontoffel Pock
Playhouse
Ages 2–6
    Adaptation, Animation, Language Arts

Halloween Is Grinch Night
Playhouse
Ages 2–6
    Adaptation, Animation, Language Arts

The Hoober-Bloob Highway
Playhouse
Ages 2–6
    Adaptation, Animation, Language Arts

Hop on Pop
Random House
Ages 2–6
    Adaptation, Animation, Language Arts

Horton Hears a Who/The Grinch Who Stole Christmas
MGM/UA
Ages 4–8
    Adaptation, Animation, Language Arts

The Lorax
Playhouse
Ages 2–6
    Adaptation, Animation, Environment, Language Arts

One Fish Two Fish Red Fish Blue Fish
Random House
Ages 2–6
    Adaptation, Animation, Language Arts

The Dream Is Alive
Finley-Holiday
Family (7 and up)
    Reference, Science, Travel

Eco, You and Simon, Too!
Centerpoint Communications Group
Ages 3–8
    Environment, Language Arts, Music, Reference

The Electric Grandmother
LCA
Ages 8–12
    Adaptation, Family, Fantasy (8 & Up), Language Arts

The Elephant's Child
Random House
Series: Rabbit Ears Productions
Ages 4–8
    Adaptation, Animals, Animation, Language Arts

ENCYCLOPEDIA BROWN
(2 titles)
Hi-Tops
Ages 4–12
    Adaptation

Eyes of Amaryllis
Vestron
Ages 8 & up
    Adaptation, Coming of Age, Fantasy (8 and Up), History

Fables of Harry Allard
Includes "Miss Nelson Is Missing," "It's So Nice To Have a Wolf around the House"
LCA
Ages 6–8
    Animation, Adaptation, Language Arts

Family Circle Presents Storyland Theatre (Vols. 1–6)
Features Rafe Martin, Laura Simms, Jay O'Callahan
Paperback Visual Publishing
Ages 4–10
    Adaptation, Fairy Tales & Legends, Language Arts

First Christmas
Golden Book
Ages 3–10
    Animation

The Fisherman and His Wife
SVS

124 Suggested Video Titles

Series: Rabbit Ears Productions
Ages 7–10
    Adaptation, Animation, Fantasy (8 & Up), Language Arts

Five Lionni Classics
Random House
Ages 4–10
    Adaptation, Animation

Five Stories for the Very Young
Includes "Changes, Changes," "Harold's Fairy Tale," "Whistle for Willie," "Caps for Sale," "Drummer Hoff"
CC Studios
Series: Children's Circle
Ages 3–6
    Adaptation, Animation, Language Arts

The Flight of the Navigator
Disney
Ages 5–12

Frog
Orion
Series: WonderWorks
Ages 7–12
    Fairy Tales & Legends, Travel

The Frog King
Davenport Films
Series: From the Brothers Grimm
Ages 5 and up
    Adaptation, Fairy Tales & Legends, Language Arts

From Star Wars to Jedi: The Making of a Saga
Playhouse
Ages 8–12
    Reference

Fun in a Box: One
Includes "Ben's Dream" (ages 7 and up), "The Red Ball Express" (ages 5–12), "Fish" (ages 6–9)
Made-to-Order Productions
    Adaptation, Animation/ Live Action

Fun in a Box: Two
Includes "Howard" (ages 6–12), "Metal Dogs of India" (ages 8 and up), "American Storytelling" (ages 6 and up), "The Kinetic Sculpture of Gordon Barlow" (ages 8 and up)
Made-to-Order Productions
    Adaptation, Animation/ Live Action

Funny Stories
Includes "The Most Wonderful Egg in the World," "The Cow Who Fell in the Canal," "The Bear and the Fly," "Joey Runs Away"
CC Studios
Series: Children's Circle
Ages 3–7
    Adaptation, Animals, Animation, Language Arts

Gandhi
RCA/Columbia
Ages 10 and up
    Biography, History, Multiculture

Get Ready, Get Set, Grow!
Bullfrog Films
Ages 7 and up
    Environment, Reference, Science

Gift of the Whales
Miramar
Ages 6–12
    Animals, Coming of Age, Environment, Multiculture, Science

A Girl of the Limberlost
Public Media Video
Series: WonderWorks
Ages 8–14
> Adaptation, Coming of Age, Environment, Family

Goggles
Coronet/MTI
Ages 4–7
> Animation, Multiculture

The Golden Seal
Nelson
Ages 6 and up
> Animals, Environment

GREAT EVENTS VIDEO LIBRARY (20 titles)
1950–1969
Bennett Marine Video
Ages 8 and up
> Animals, Biography, Environment, Fine Arts, History, Language Arts, Multiculture, Music, Reference, Science

Gregory and the Terrible Eater/ Gila Monsters Meet You at the Airport
Vestron
Series: Reading Rainbow
Ages 4–10
> Animals, Animation/Live Action, Language Arts, Travel

Hansel and Gretel
Davenport Films
Series: From the Brothers Grimm
Ages 5 and up
> Adaptation, Fairy Tales & Legends, Language Arts, Multiculture

Hansel and Gretel (opera)
Paramount
Ages 5 and up
> Adaptation, Fairy Tales & Legends, Fine Arts, Music

Hansel and Gretel (puppets)
Vestron
Ages 5–11
> Adaptation, Fairy Tales & Legends

Happy Birthday, Moon and Other Stories
Also includes "Peter's Chair," "The Napping House," "The Three Little Pigs," "The Owl and the Pussycat"
CC Studios
Series: Children's Circle
Ages 3–7
> Adaptation, Animation, Language Arts

The Harlem Globetrotters
Fries
Ages 6 and up
> Biography, Reference

Here We Go (Vols. 1–2)
Just for Kids
Ages 4–8
> Reference, Travel

Herschel Walker's Fitness Challenges for Kids
HPG
Ages 7 and up
> Reference

Hey, What about Me
KIDVIDZ
Ages 4–8
> Family, Reference

The Hideaways
Warner
Ages 6 and up
> Adaptation, Family, Fine Arts, Language Arts

Higglety Pigglety Pop! (opera)
HomeVision
Ages 5–12
    Adaptation, Fine Arts, Music

Hiroshima Maiden
Public Media Video
Series: WonderWorks
Ages 8 and up
    Coming of Age, Family, History, Multiculture

Hockey Night
Family Home Entertainment
Series: WonderWorks
Ages 6 and up
    Family

Home Alone
Hi-Tops
Ages 7–14
    Reference

Homer Price Stories
Includes "The Doughnuts," "The Case of the Cosmic Comic"
CC Studios
Series: Children's Circle
Ages 5–9
    Adaptation, Animation, Language Arts

How the Leopard Got His Spots
SVS
Series: Rabbit Ears Productions
Ages 5–9
    Adaptation, Animals, Animation, Fairy Tales & Legends, Language Arts

How the Rhinoceros Got His Skin/How the Camel Got His Hump
SVS
Series: Rabbit Ears Productions
Ages 5–10
    Adaptation, Animals, Animation, Fairy Tales & Legends, Language Arts

How To Be a Perfect Person in Just Three Days
Public Media Video
Series: WonderWorks
Ages 5–12
    Language Arts

How To Draw Comics the Marvel Way
New World
Ages 8–14
    Reference

HUBLEY STUDIO ANIMATION
(6 titles)
Series includes *Ages of Humankind; Cosmic Eye; Delicate Thread; Flight of Fancy; Of Stars and Men; Urbanscape*
Disney
Ages 8 and up
    Animation, Multiculture

THE HUMAN RACE CLUB
(3 titles)
Series includes *A Story about Fights between Brothers and Sisters; A Story about Making Friends; A Story about Self-Esteem*
Kids Media Group
Just for Kids
Ages 6–8
    Adaptation, Animation, Family

Humphrey the Lost Whale
GPN/Lancit Media
Series: Reading Rainbow
Ages 4–8
    Adaptation, Environment, Science

I Can Dance
JCI
Ages 6–12
    Fine Arts, Music, Reference

The Incredible Journey
Disney
Ages 5–12
    Animals, Travel

Inside the Labyrinth
Nelson
Ages 7–14
    Reference

Island of the Blue Dolphins
MCA
Ages 8–14
    Adaptation, Biography, Environment, History, Language Arts, Multiculture

Ivanhoe
MGM/UA
Ages 8 and up
    Adaptation, History, Language Arts

Jack and the Beanstalk
Hanna Barbera
Ages 5–12
    Adaptation, Animation/Live Action, Fairy Tales & Legends, Music

Jack and the Dentist's Daughter
Davenport Films
Series: From the Brothers Grimm
Ages 6 and up
    Adaptation, Fairy Tales & Legends, Language Arts

Jacob Have I Loved
Public Media Video
Series: WonderWorks
Ages 9 and up
    Adaptation, Coming of Age, Family

Jacob Two-Two Meets the Hooded Fang
Vestron
Ages 4–8
    Adaptation

JIM HENSON'S PLAY-ALONG VIDEO (4 titles)
Series includes *Hey, You're as Funny as Fozzie Bear* (ages 5–9), *Neat Stuff To Know and To Do* (ages 6–10), *Wow, You're a Cartoonist* (ages 5–11), *Sing-Along, Dance-Along, Do-Along* (ages 3–9)
Warner/Lorimar
    Music, Reference

Joe Scruggs: Joe's First Video
HPG
Ages 4–9
    Animation/Live Action, Language Arts, Music

John and Julie
Family Home Entertainment
Ages 7 and up
    History, Multiculture

The Journey of Natty Gann
Disney
Ages 8 and up
    Adaptation, Coming of Age, Family, History

The Jungle Book
Disney
Ages 4–10
    Adaptation, Animals, Animation, Language Arts, Multiculture

The Jungle Book
Embassy (black & white)
Roach (color)
Ages 6 and up
    Adaptation, Animals, Language Arts, Multiculture

Kids Ask about War
PBS Video
Ages 8–12
    History, Multiculture, Reference

Kids for Safety
Classic Telepublishing
Ages 7–14
   Reference

Kids in Action
Playhouse
Ages 4–12
   Language Arts, Music,
   Reference

KIDSONGS (2 titles)
Series includes *I'd Like To Teach the World To Sing; Sing Out America*
ViewMaster
Ages 4–8
   Music, Travel

Kim
MGM/UA
Ages 6 and up
   Adaptation, History,
   Language Arts, Multiculture

The Land of Faraway
Starmaker
Ages 5–12
   Adaptation

Lantern Hill
Buena Vista
Series: WonderWorks
Ages 6–12
   Coming of Age, Family,
   Language Arts

Lassie Come Home
MGM/UA
All ages
   Adaptation, Animal, Family

The Legend of Sleepy Hollow
SVS
Series: Rabbit Ears Productions
Ages 7–12
   Adaptation, Animation,
   Fairy Tales & Legends,
   Language Arts

Let's Be Friends: Tickle Tune Typhoon
Just for Kids
Ages 4–10
   Environment, Music

Let's Get a Move On
KIDVIDZ
Ages 4–10
   Family, Reference

Lift Off!
Premiere Home Video
Ages 8 and up
   History, Reference, Science,
   Travel

The Light Princess
Playhouse
Ages 5–10
   Adaptation,
   Animation/Live Action,
   Language Arts

Lights
Ergo Media
Ages 6–12
   Animation, History,
   Reference

A Link with Nature
The Oasis Project/Music for
   Little People
All ages
   Animals, Environment,
   Music

The Lion, the Witch and the Wardrobe
Vestron
Ages 6–12
   Adaptation, Animation,
   Language Arts

Little League's Official How-To-Play Baseball by Video
MasterVision
Age 8–12
   Reference

Alphabetical List   129

Little Lord Fauntleroy
Family Home Entertainment
Ages 8–14
    Adaptation, Family, History

The Little Match Girl
Family Home Entertainment
Ages 4–9
    Adaptation, Animation,
    Language Arts, Fairy Tales
    & Legends, Multiculture

The Little Princess
Active, Playhouse
Ages 6–12
    Adaptation, Language Arts,
    Music

The Little Princess
Public Media Video
Series: WonderWorks
Ages 5 and up
    Adaptation, History,
    Language Arts

Little Women
MGM/UA
Ages 5 and up
    Adaptation, Biography,
    Family, History, Language
    Arts

Look What I Made: Paper Playthings and Gifts
Pacific Arts
Ages 6–10
    Reference

Looking for Miracles
Disney
Series: WonderWorks
Ages 7–14
    Coming of Age, Family,
    History, Language Arts

LORNE GREENE'S NEW WILDERNESS (2 titles)
Series includes *The Ascent of the Chimps; A Love Story: The Canadian Goose*
Prism
Ages 5 and up
    Animals, Environment,
    Reference, Science

Lyle, Lyle Crocodile: The Musical
Hi-Tops
Ages 4–12
    Adaptation, Animals,
    Animation, Music

MACMILLAN VIDEO ALMANAC FOR KIDS (2 titles)
Series includes *Inside Fun* (ages 10–14), *Rainy Day Games* (ages 6–10)
VPI, Inc.
    Language Arts,
    Multiculture,
    Reference, Science

Madeline: The Musical
Hi-Tops
Ages 6 and under
    Adaptation, Animation,
    Language Arts, Music,
    Travel

Madeline's Rescue
Also includes "Madeline and the Bad Hat," "Madeline and the Gypsies"
CC Studios
Series: Children's Circle
Ages 4–9
    Adaptation, Animation,
    Language Arts

Maestro's Company, Vol. 1
(opera)
Includes "The Barber of Seville," "La Traviata"
Video Artists International
Ages 5–12
    Fine Arts, Music, Travel

Maestro's Company, Vol. 2
(opera)

Includes "Rigoletto,"
"Hansel and Gretel"
Video Artists International
Ages 5–12
    Fine Arts, Travel, Music

Maia: A Dinosaur Grows Up
Running Press
Ages 3–6
    Adaptation, Animals,
    Animation, History, Science

Man of the Trees: The Life of Richard St. Barbe
Music for Little People
Ages 7 and up
    Biography, Environment,
    Multiculture, Travel

The Man Who Didn't Wash for Seven Years
Davenport Films
Series: From the Brothers Grimm
Ages 5 and up
    Adaptation, Fairy Tales &
    Legends, Language Arts

The Maurice Sendak Library
Includes "The Nutshell Kids,"
"In the Night Kitchen,"
"Where the Wild Things Are,"
"Getting To Know Maurice Sendak"
CC Studios
Series: Children's Circle
All ages
    Adaptation, Animation,
    Language Arts, Music

Medicine Hat Stallion
Vestron
Ages 8 and up
    Adaptation, Animals,
    Coming of Age, History,
    Multiculture

Merlin and the Dragons
Hi-Tops
Series: Stories To Remember
Ages 6–12
    Adaptation, Animation,
    Fairy Tales & Legends,
    Language Arts

The Mighty Pawns
Public Media Video
Series: WonderWorks
Ages 8–12
    Coming of Age, Multiculture

Mike Mulligan and His Steam Shovel and Other Stories
Also includes "Burt Dow: Deep-Water Man," "Moon Man"
CC Studios
Series: Children's Circle
Ages 3–9
    Adaptation, Animation,
    Language Arts

Miracle at Moreaux
Public Media Video
Series: WonderWorks
Ages 6 and up
    Adaptation, History,
    Multiculture

Miracle Down Under
Disney
Series: WonderWorks
Ages 5 and up
    Family, Travel

The Miracle Worker
MGM/UA
Ages 8 and up
    Adaptation, Biography,
    Family, History

Molly's Pilgrim
Phoenix
Ages 5 and up
    Adaptation, History,
    Multiculture

More Dinosaurs
Twin Tower

Alphabetical List 131

Ages 4–9
    Animals, Science

Morris Goes to School
Churchill
Ages 5–7
    Adaptation, Animals,
    Animation, Language Arts

Mowgli's Brothers
Family Home Entertainment
Ages 5–9
    Adaptation, Animals,
    Animation, Language Arts

My Family and Other Animals
(2 tapes)
Playhouse
Ages 5–12
    Adaptation, Animals,
    Biography, Environment,
    Family, Multiculture, Travel

The Mysterious Tadpole and Other Stories
Also includes "The Five Chinese Brothers," "Jonah and the Great Fish," "The Wizard"
CC Studios
Series: Children's Circle
Ages 3–8
    Adaptation, Animals,
    Animation, Language Arts

Mystery Island
VidAmerica
Ages 8 and up
    Family, Fantasy (8 & Up)

NATIONAL FILM BOARD OF CANADA (3 titles)
Series includes *Every Child and Four Other Titles for Family Enjoyment*; *Sea Dream and Four Other Titles for Family Enjoyment*; *The Tender Tale of Cinderella Penguin and Four Other Titles for Family Enjoyment*

Smarty Pants
All ages
    Animation, Fine Arts,
    Language Arts

NATIONAL GEOGRAPHIC
(5 titles)
Series includes *African Wildlife* (ages 5 and up), *Rain Forest* (ages 7 and up), *Save the Panda* (ages 8 and up), *The Sharks* (ages 8 and up), *The Tropical Kingdom of Belize* (ages 8 and up)
National Geographic Society
Vestron
    Animals, Reference, Science

National Velvet
MGM/UA
Ages 6 and up
    Adaptation, Animals, Family

Necessary Parties
Public Media
Series: WonderWorks
Ages 7 and up
    Adaptation, Family

Never Cry Wolf
Disney
Ages 6 and up
    Adaptation, Animals,
    Environment

The NeverEnding Story
Warner
Ages 8 and up
    Adaptation, Fantasy (8 & Up), Language Arts

Newton's Apple
PBS Video
Ages 8–12
    Animals, Reference, Science

Noah's Ark
Hi-Tops
Series: Stories To Remember

132 Suggested Video Titles

Ages 4–8
    Adaptation, Animals, Animation, History, Language Arts

Norman the Doorman and Other Stories
Also includes "Brave Irene," "Lentil"
CC Studios
Series: Children's Circle
Ages 4–9
    Adaptation, Animation, Language Arts

Nursery Rhymes
Family Home Entertainment
Ages 3–6
    Adaptation, Animation/Live Action, Language Arts

The Nutcracker: A Fantasy on Ice
Vidmark
Family
    Adaptation, Fairy Tales & Legends, Fine Arts, Music

The Nutcracker: The Motion Picture (ballet)
KVC
Family
    Adaptation, Fine Arts, Music

Ocean Symphony
MCA
Ages 6 and up
    Animals, Science, Reference

Old Yeller
Disney
Ages 5–14
    Adaptation, Animals

Oliver!
RCA/Columbia
Ages 6 and up
    Adaptation, History, Music

Oliver Twist
Paramount
Ages 8 and up
    Adaptation, History, Language Arts

1-2-3 MAGIC (2 titles)
Child Management
Adult
    Reference

Out of Time
Family Express
Ages 6–10
    Family, History

Owl Moon and Other Stories
Also includes "The Caterpillar and the Polliwog," "Hot Hippo," "Time of Wonder"
CC Studios
Series: Children's Circle
Ages 4–9
    Adaptation, Animals, Animation, Language Arts

Paul Bunyan
SVS
Series: Rabbit Ears Productions
Ages 5–12
    Adaptation, Animation, Fairy Tales & Legends, Language Arts

Pecos Bill
SVS
Series: Rabbit Ears Productions
Ages 4–12
    Adaptation, Animation, Fairy Tales & Legends, Language Arts

Pegasus
Hi-Tops
Series: Stories To Remember
Ages 5–9
    Adaptation, Animation, Fairy Tales & Legends, Language Arts

Alphabetical List   133

PIPPI LONGSTOCKING
(4 titles)
Series includes *Pippi Goes on Board; Pippi in the South Seas; Pippi Longstocking; Pippi on the Run*
VidAmerica
Ages 4–8
    Adaptation, Multiculture, Travel

The Point
Vestron
Ages 4 and up
    Animation, Music

Pollyanna
Disney
Ages 4–12
    Adaptation, Family

The Princess Bride
Nelson
Ages 8–12
    Adaptation, Fantasy (8 & Up)

Pyramid
PBS Video
Ages 8 and up
    Adaptation, Animation, Fine Arts, History, Language Arts, Reference

THE RAMONA SERIES
(10 titles)
Series includes *The Bad Day; Goodbye, Hello; The Great Hair Argument; The Mystery Meal; The New Pajamas; The Patient; The Perfect Day; The Rainy Sunday; Siblingitis; Squeakerfoot*
Warner
Ages 4–12
    Adaptation, Family

Really Rosie
CC Studios
Ages 4–10
    Animation, Music

The Red Balloon
Nelson, Budget Video
Ages 4–12
    Adaptation

Red Riding Hood and Goldilocks
SVS
Series: Rabbit Ears Productions
Ages 5–10
    Adaptation, Animation, Fairy Tales & Legends, Language Arts

The Red Shoes
Family Home Entertainment
Ages 4–9
    Adaptation, Animation, Multiculture, Music

The Reluctant Dragon
Disney
Ages 4–9
    Adaptation, Animation

Richard Scarry's Best Alphabet Video Ever
Random House
Ages 2–6
    Animation, Language Arts

Richard Scarry's Best Counting Video Ever
Random House
Ages 2–6
    Animation

Richard Scarry's Tales
Golden Book
Ages 2–6
    Animation, Language Arts

Rikki-Tikki-Tavi
Family Home Entertainment
Ages 4–9
    Adaptation, Animation, Language Arts

The Robert McCloskey Library
Includes "Lentil," "Make Way for

134 Suggested Video Titles

Ducklings," "Blueberries for Sal," "Time of Wonder," "Burt Dow: Deep-Water Man," "Getting To Know Robert McCloskey"
CC Studios
Series: Children's Circle
All ages
  Adaptation, Animation, Language Arts

RUB A DUB DUB (2 titles)
Hi-Tops
Ages 3–7
  Animation, Language Arts

Rudyard Kipling's Classic Stories
Includes "How the Elephant Got His Trunk," "How the First Letter Was Written," "How the Whale Got His Throat"
LCA
Ages 4–10
  Adaptation, Animals, Animation, Fairy Tales & Legends, Language Arts

Rudyard Kipling's Just So Stories
Includes "How the Whale Got His Throat," "The Crab That Played with the Sea," "How the Leopard Got His Spots," "The Cat That Walked by Himself," "How the Rhinoceros Got His Skin"
Vestron
Ages 4–7
  Adaptation, Animals, Fairy Tales & Legends, Language Arts

Rumplestiltskin
Family Home Entertainment
Ages 4–7
  Adaptation, Fairy Tales & Legends, Language Arts

Runaway
Public Media Video
Series: WonderWorks
Ages 8–12
  Adaptation, Coming of Age, Language Arts

RUNAWAY ISLAND (4 titles)
Series includes *The Quest for James McLeod; The Exiles; The Bushranger; Treasure of the Conquistadors*
SVS
Ages 8 and up
  Language Arts

Run, Rebecca, Run!
VidAmerica
Series: WonderWorks
Ages 6 and up
  Multiculture

Sadako and the Thousand Paper Cranes
Informed Democracy
Ages 8 and up
  Animation, History, Language Arts, Multiculture, Reference

Samson and Sally: The Song of the Whales
Just for Kids
Ages 5–9
  Adaptation, Animals, Animation, Environment

Sarah and the Squirrel
Playhouse
Ages 9–12
  Animation, History

Say It by Signing
Crown
Ages 9 and up
  Language Arts, Reference

SCHOLASTIC BLUE RIBBON STORYBOOK VIDEO (2 titles)
Series includes, in *Volume 1*, "The Three Billy-Goats Gruff," "The

Little Red Hen"; in *Volume 2*, "Harold and the Purple Crayon," "The Brementown Musicians"
Warner
Ages 3–7
    Adaptation, Animals, Fairy Tales & Legends, Language Arts

The Secret Garden
Playhouse
Ages 5–10
    Adaptation, Family, Language Arts

The Secret of NIMH
MGM/UA
Ages 6–12
    Adaptation, Animals, Animation, Family

Shalom Sesame (5 titles)
Series includes *Jerusalem; Kibbutz; The Land of Israel; The People of Israel; Tel Aviv*
Children's Television Workshop
Ages 6–8
    Multiculture, Reference, Travel

SHIRLEY TEMPLE (4 titles)
Series includes *Curly Top; Heidi; The Little Princess; Rebecca of Sunnybrook Farm*
Playhouse
All ages
    Adaptation, Language Arts

Sign Me a Story
Random House
Ages 4–10
    Adaptation, Language Arts, Reference

Silent Mouse
Interama
Family
    Language Arts, Music, Travel

The Silent One
VidAmerica
Series: WonderWorks
Ages 6 and up
    Animals, Multiculture

Sleeping Beauty on Ice
Kultur
Ages 4–8
    Adaptation, Fairy Tales & Legends, Fine Arts, Language Arts, Music

Smile for Auntie and Other Stories
Also includes "Make Way for Ducklings," "The Snowy Day," "Wynken, Blynken and Nod"
CC Studios
Series: Children's Circle
Ages 3–10
    Adaptation, Animation, Language Arts

The Snowman
CC Studios
Series: Children's Circle
All ages
    Adaptation, Animation, Language Arts

Soldier Jack
Davenport Films
Series: From the Brothers Grimm
Ages 8 and up
    Adaptation, Fairy Tales & Legends, Language Arts

Sometimes I Wonder
Media Ventures
Ages 5 and up
    Animals, Family

Sounder
Paramount
Ages 10 and up

Adaptation, History,
Multiculture

Squiggles, Dots and Lines
KIDVIDZ
Ages 6 and up
    Reference

Starlight Hotel
Republic
Ages 9 and up
    Adaptation, Coming of Age

Steadfast Tin Soldier
Random House
Ages 4–10
    Animation, Fairy Tales &
    Legends

STORIES AND FABLES
(19 titles)
Disney
Ages 6–12
    Adaptation, Fairy Tales &
    Legends, Language Arts

STORIES OF AMERICAN INDIAN CULTURE (3 titles)
Series includes *Hawk, I'm Your Brother*; *The Other Way To Listen*; *The Way To Start a Day*
Best Film & Video
Ages 6–12
    Adaptation, Multiculture

The Story about Ping and Other Stories
Also includes "Charlie Needs a Cloak," "The Beast of Monsieur Racine"
CC Studios
Series: Children's Circle
Ages 3–9
    Adaptation, Animation,
    Language Arts

The Story of the Dancing Frog
Family Home Entertainment
Ages 4 and up
    Animation, Adaptation,
    Music

Strega Nonna and Other Stories
Also includes "Tikki Tikki Tembo," "The Foolish Frog," "A Story—A Story"
CC Studios
Series: Children's Circle
Ages 4–8
    Adaptation, Animals,
    Animation, Language Arts

Sweet 15
Public Media Video
Series: WonderWorks
Ages 12 and up
    Coming of Age, Family,
    Multiculture

Swiss Family Robinson
Disney
Ages 4–12
    Adaptation, Family,
    Language Arts

Sword in the Stone
Disney
Ages 4–8
    Adaptation, Fairy Tales &
    Legends, Language Arts

The Tailor of Gloucester
SVS
Series: Rabbit Ears Productions
Ages 4–10
    Adaptation, Animation,
    Fairy Tales & Legends,
    Language Arts

The Tale of Mr. Jeremy Fisher and The Tale of Peter Rabbit
SVS
Series: Rabbit Ears Productions
Ages 3–7
    Adaptation, Animals,
    Animation, Language Arts

Tales of Beatrix Potter (ballet)
HBO
Ages 6 and up
>Adaptation, Animals, Fine Arts, Music

The Talking Parcels
Simon & Schuster
Ages 6–12
>Adaptation, Animation

TALL TALES AND LEGENDS (5 titles)
Series includes *Annie Oakley; Casey at the Bat; Darlin' Clementine; Johnny Appleseed; Pecos Bill, King of the Cowboys*
Playhouse
Ages 6–12
>Adaptation, Fairy Tales & Legends, Language Arts

Teach Me To Dance
Films, Inc.
Ages 7–14
>Fine Arts, Language Arts, Multiculture

Teeny-Tiny and the Witch-Woman and Other Scary Stories
Also includes "King of the Cats," "The Rainbow Serpent," "A Dark, Dark Tale"
CC Studios
Series: Children's Circle
Ages 4–10
>Adaptation, Animation, Language Arts

TELL ME WHY (18 titles)
Series includes *Americana; Anatomy and Genetics; Animals and Arachnids; Beginnings: Civilization and Government; Birds and Rodents; Fish, Shellfish and Other Underwater Life; Flowers, Plants and Trees; Gems, Metals and Minerals; A Healthy Body; Life Forms, Animals and Animal Oddities; Mammals; Medicine; Prehistoric Animals, Reptiles and Amphibians; Science, Sound and Energy; Space, Earth and Atmosphere; Sports and Games; Water and Weather*
Tell Me Why Video
Ages 6–14
>Adaptation, Animals, History, Reference, Science

Thomas Edison: The Boy Who Lit Up the World
VidAmerica
Ages 7–12
>Biography, History

The Three Billy Goats Gruff/ The Three Little Pigs
SVS
Series: Rabbit Ears Productions
Ages 4–9
>Adaptation, Animals, Animation, Fairy Tales & Legends, Language Arts

The Three Musketeers
MGM/UA
Ages 7 and up
>Adaptation, Language Arts

The Three Robbers and Other Stories
Also includes "Fourteen Rats and a Rat-Catcher," "The Island of the Skog," "Leopold the See-Through Crumbpicker"
CC Studios
Series: Children's Circle
Ages 4–10
>Adaptation, Animals, Animation, Language Arts

3-2-1 CONTACT EXTRA (3 titles)
Series includes *Down the Drain;*

The Rotten Truth; You Can't Grow Home Again
Children's Television Workshop
All ages
    Environment, Reference, Science

3-2-1 Contact Greatest Hits: Animal Tracks
Golden Book
Ages 4 and up
    Animation, Music

Thumbelina
RCA/Columbia
Ages 4–10
    Adaptation, Animation, Fairy Tales & Legends, Language Arts

Thumbelina
SVS
Series: Rabbit Ears Productions
Ages 3–7
    Adaptation, Animation, Fairy Tales & Legends, Language Arts

TIMELINE (6 titles)
Series includes *The Vikings; The Crusades; The Mongol Empire; The Black Death; The Fall of Byzantium; Granada*
Zenger Video
Ages 11 and up
    Biography, History, Multiculture, Reference, Travel

The Tin Soldier
Hi-Tops
Ages 3–12
    Adaptation, Animation, Fairy Tales & Legends

To Kill a Mockingbird
MCA
Ages 9 and up
    Adaptation, Family, History, Language Arts, Multiculture

Tom Thumb
MGM/UA
Ages 6 and up
    Adaptation, Fairy Tales & Legends, Language Arts, Music

Tommy Tricker and the Stamp Traveller
Family Home Entertainment
Ages 5–14
    Travel

The Tortoise and the Hare and Hill of Fire
Vestron
Series: Reading Rainbow
Ages 4–9
    Adaptation, History

Treasure Island
MGM/UA
Ages 7 and up
    Adaptation, History, Language Arts

A Tree Grows in Brooklyn
Playhouse
Ages 8 and up
    Adaptation, Family, History, Language Arts

Tuck Everlasting
Vestron
Ages 8 and Up
    Adaptation, Family, Fantasy (8 & Up)

Twelve Months
RCA/Columbia
Ages 5–9
    Adaptation, Animation, Fairy Tales & Legends

The Ugly Duckling
Random House

Series: Rabbit Ears Productions
Ages 5–10
    Adaptation, Animation,
    Fairy Tales & Legends,
    Language Arts

The Ugly Duckling and Other Classic Fairytales
Also includes "The Stonecutter," "The Swineherd"
CC Studios
Series: Children's Circle
Ages 4–9
    Adaptation, Animation,
    Fairy Tales & Legends,
    Language Arts

THE UNDERSEA WORLD OF JACQUES COUSTEAU (6 titles)
Series includes *The Singing Whale; The Unsinkable Sea Otter; The Smile of the Walrus; A Sound of Dolphins; Octopus-Octopus; The Dragons of Galapagos*
Pacific Arts
Ages 8 and up
    Animals, Environment,
    Science

The Velveteen Rabbit
Family Home Entertainment
Ages 4–10
    Adaptation, Animation,
    Language Arts

The Velveteen Rabbit
Random House
Series: Rabbit Ears Productions
Ages 3–6
    Adaptation, Animation,
    Language Arts

The Velveteen Rabbit
Running Press
Ages 3–6
    Adaptation, Animation,
    Language Arts

The Very Merry Cricket
Family Home Entertainment
Ages 4–8
    Adaptation, Animals,
    Animation

VIDEO FLASH CARDS (8 titles)
Spell Well (4 titles)
Math (4 titles)
Child's Play
Ages 7–12
    Reference

The Video Guide to Stamp Collecting
Premiere
Ages 7 and up
    Reference

THE VIDEO LETTER FROM JAPAN (6 titles)
Asia Society
Ages 7–14
    Family, Multiculture,
    Reference, Travel

VIDEOTOURS (11 titles)
Great America Series (6 titles)
    includes *Audubon Zoo; Columbus Zoo; Mystic Seaport; Old Sturbridge Village; San Diego Wild Animal Park; San Diego Zoo*
VideoTours
Ages 6 and up
    Animals, Environment,
    History, Reference, Science,
    Travel
History Collection (3 titles)
    includes *The Newport Mansions; Old Salem; Plimoth Plantation*
VideoTours
Ages 7 and up
    History, Reference, Travel
Science/Nature Collection (2 titles)
    includes *American Museum of Natural History; Monterey Bay Aquarium*

140 Suggested Video Titles

VideoTours
Ages 6 and up
    Environment, Reference, Science, Travel

Walking on Air
Public Media Video
Series: WonderWorks
Ages 6–12
    Science

A Waltz through the Hills
Public Media Video
Series: WonderWorks
Ages 6–12
    Family, Multiculture

Watership Down
Warner
Ages 8 and up
    Animals, Animation, Fantasy (8 & Up)

What's a Good Story?
  Beauty and the Beast
Coronet/MTI
Ages 8 and up
    Animation, Language Arts

What's Happening To Me?
Starmaker
Ages 10 and up
    Adaptation, Animation, Reference, Science

What's Under My Bed and Other Creepy Stories
Also includes "The Three Robbers," "Georgie," "Teeny-Tiny and the Witch-Woman"
CC Studios
Series: Children's Circle
Ages 4–9
    Adaptation, Animation, Language Arts

When the Whales Came
CBS/Fox
Ages 9 and up
    Animals, Coming of Age, Environment, Multiculture

Where Did I Come From?
LCA
Ages 7 and up
    Animation, Science, Reference

WHERE IN THE WORLD
(3 titles)
Series includes *Kids Explore Alaska; Kids Explore Kenya; Kids Explore Mexico*
Encounter Video
Ages 7–12
    Animals, Environment, Reference, Travel

Where the Red Fern Grows
Vestron
Ages 8 and up
    Adaptation, Animals, Coming of Age, Family, Language Arts

Where the Wild Things Are
  (opera)
HomeVision
Ages 6 and up
    Adaptation, Music

The White Seal
Family Home Entertainment
Ages 4–9
    Adaptation, Animals, Animation, Fairy Tales & Legends, Language Arts

Who Has Seen the Wind?
Embassy Home Video
Series: WonderWorks
Ages 8 and up
    Coming of Age, History

Who's Afraid of Opera?
Kultur

Ages 5 and up
    Fine Arts, Music, Reference

Wilbur and Orville: First To Fly
VidAmerica
Ages 7–12
    Biography, History

The Wild Pony
Vestron
Series: WonderWorks
Ages 7–12
    Coming of Age

Will Rogers: Champion of the People
VidAmerica
Ages 7–12
    Biography, History

The Wind in the Willows (4 tapes)
HBO/Thorn-EMI
Ages 4–8
    Adaptation, Animals,
    Family, Fantasy (8 & Up)

The Witches
Warner
Ages 8 and up
    Adaptation, Family, Fantasy
    (8 & up)

The Wizard of Oz
MGM/UA
Ages 4 and up
    Adaptation, Music

A World Alive
Sea Studios
All Ages
    Environment, Reference,
    Science

The World of Anne Frank
Ergo Media
Ages 9–12
    Biography, History,
    Reference

Yankee Doodle Cricket
Family Home Entertainment
Ages 4–8
    Animals, Animation,
    History

The Yearling
MGM/UA
Ages 7 and up
    Adaptation, Animals,
    Coming of Age, Family

YOU CAN CHOOSE (4 titles)
Series includes *Dealing with Feelings; Being Responsible; Saying No; Cooperation*
Live Wire
Ages 8–12
    Reference

The Young Magician
Family Home Entertainment
Ages 5–14
    Travel

Video Titles by Category

ADAPTATION

ABC (Dr. Seuss titles)
Abel's Island
The Adventures of Huckleberry Finn
The Adventures of Robin Hood
Alice in Wonderland
Amahl and the Night Visitors (opera)
The Amazing Bone and Other Stories
American Storytelling Stories Series
Animal Stories
Animal Talk
Anne of Avonlea
Anne of Green Gables
Arthur's Eyes

142 Suggested Video Titles

Ashpet: An American Cinderella
The Autobiography of Miss Jane Pittman
Babar titles
Bank Street Read-Along Story Videos Series
Beauty and the Beast (Hi-Tops)
Beauty and the Beast (Nelson)
The Black Stallion
The Black Stallion Returns
Born Free
The Box of Delights
The Bridge to Terabithia
The Brothers Lionheart
The Butter Battle Book (Dr. Seuss)
Captains Courageous
Castle
The Cat in the Hat (Dr. Seuss)
The Cat in the Hat Comes Back (Dr. Seuss)
Cathedral
Charlotte's Web
A Child's Christmas in Wales
Chitty Chitty Bang Bang
A Christmas Carol
Christmas Stories
Cinderella: Rodgers and Hammerstein
Classic Fairy Tales
Clifford's Fun Series
A Connecticut Yankee at King Arthur's Court
Corduroy and Other Bear Stories
The Cricket in Times Square (3 titles)
David Copperfield
The Devil and Daniel Mouse
The Diary of Anne Frank
Diggin Up Dinosaurs
Doctor De Soto and Other Stories
Dr. Seuss: *Dr. Seuss Festival* (Dr. Seuss); *Dr. Seuss on the Loose* (Dr. Seuss)
The Electric Grandmother
The Elephant's Child
Encyclopedia Brown

Eyes of Amaryllis
Fables of Harry Allard
Family Circle Presents Storyland Theatre
The Fisherman and His Wife
Five Lionni Classics
Five Stories for the Very Young
Frog
The Frog King
Fun in a Box 1
Fun in a Box 2
Funny Stories
A Girl of the Limberlost
The Grinch Grinches Cat in the Hat/Pontoffel Pock (Dr. Seuss)
Halloween Is Grinch Night (Dr. Seuss)
Hansel and Gretel
Hansel and Gretel (opera)
Hansel and Gretel (puppets)
Happy Birthday, Moon and Other Stories
The Hideaways
Higglety Pigglety Pop! (opera)
Homer Price Stories
The Hoober-Bloob Highway (Dr. Seuss)
Hop on Pop (Dr. Seuss)
Horton Hears a Who/The Grinch Who Stole Christmas (Dr. Seuss)
How the Leopard Got His Spots
How the Rhinoceros Got His Skin/How the Camel Got His Hump
The Human Race Club Series
Humphrey the Lost Whale
Island of the Blue Dolphins
Ivanhoe
Jack and the Beanstalk
Jack and the Dentist's Daughter
Jacob Have I Loved
Jacob Two-Two Meets the Hooded Fang
The Journey of Natty Gann
The Jungle Book (Disney)
The Jungle Book (Embassy)

Kim
The Land of Faraway
Lassie Come Home
The Legend of Sleepy Hollow
The Light Princess
The Lion, the Witch and
 the Wardrobe
Little Lord Fauntleroy
The Little Match Girl
The Little Princess
 (Active, Playhouse)
The Little Princess
 (Public Media Video)
Little Women
The Lorax (Dr. Seuss)
Lyle, Lyle Crocodile: The Musical
Madeline: The Musical
Madeline's Rescue
Maia: A Dinosaur Grows Up
The Man Who Didn't Wash for
 Seven Years
The Maurice Sendak Library
Medicine Hat Stallion
Merlin and the Dragons
Mike Mulligan and His Steam
 Shovel and Other Stories
Miracle at Moreaux
The Miracle Worker
Molly's Pilgrim
Morris Goes to School
Mowgli's Brothers
My Family and Other Animals
The Mysterious Tadpole and
 Other Stories
National Velvet
Necessary Parties
Never Cry Wolf
The NeverEnding Story
Noah's Ark
Norman the Doorman and
 Other Stories
Nursery Rhymes
The Nutcracker: A Fantasy on Ice
The Nutcracker: The Motion Picture
 (ballet)
Old Yeller

Oliver!
Oliver Twist
One Fish Two Fish Red Fish
 Blue Fish (Dr. Seuss)
Owl Moon and Other Stories
Paul Bunyan
Pecos Bill
Pegasus
Pippi Longstocking Series
Pollyanna
The Princess Bride
Pyramid
The Ramona Series
The Red Balloon
Red Riding Hood and Goldilocks
The Red Shoes
The Reluctant Dragon
Rikki-Tikki-Tavi
The Robert McCloskey Library
Rudyard Kipling's Classic Stories
Rudyard Kipling's Just So Stories
Rumplestiltskin
Runaway
Samson and Sally: The Song of the
 Whales
**Scholastic Blue Ribbon
 Storybook Video** Series
The Secret Garden
The Secret of NIMH
Shirley Temple Series
Sleeping Beauty on Ice
Smile for Auntie and Other Stories
The Snowman
Soldier Jack
Sounder
Starlight Hotel
Stories and Fables
**Stories of American Indian
 Culture** Series
The Story about Ping and
 Other Stories
The Story of the Dancing Frog
Strega Nonna and Other Stories
Swiss Family Robinson
Sword in the Stone
The Tailor of Gloucester

The Tale of Mr. Jeremy Fisher and The Tale of Peter Rabbit
Tales of Beatrix Potter (ballet)
The Talking Parcels
Tall Tales and Legends Series
Tell Me Why Series
The Three Billy Goats Gruff/ The Three Little Pigs
The Three Musketeers
The Three Robbers and Other Stories
Thumbelina (RCA/Columbia)
Thumbelina (SVS)
The Tin Soldier
To Kill a Mockingbird
Tom Thumb
The Tortoise and the Hare and Hill of Fire
Treasure Island
A Tree Grows in Brooklyn
Tuck Everlasting
Twelve Months
The Ugly Duckling
The Ugly Duckling and Other Classic Fairytales
The Velveteen Rabbit (Family Home Entertainment)
The Velveteen Rabbit (Random House)
The Velveteen Rabbit (Running Press)
The Very Merry Cricket
What's Happening To Me?
What's Under My Bed and Other Creepy Stories
Where the Red Fern Grows
Where the Wild Things Are (opera)
The White Seal
The Wind in the Willows (4 titles)
The Witches
The Wizard of Oz
The Yearling

ANIMALS

Abel's Island
The Adventures of Milo and Otis
An American Tail
Animal ABCs
Animal Alphabet Series
Animal Stories
Animal Talk
Animal Wonders from Down Under Series
Animal Zoop, Vol. 2 Series
Animals in Action Series
Animals of Africa
Armchair Safaris Series
Babar titles
Baboons, Butterflies and Me
Banana, Banana, Banana Slug
The Black Stallion
The Black Stallion Returns
The Blue Frontier Series
Born Free
Bugs and Daffy's Carnival of the Animals
Carnival of the Animals (Twin Tower)
Carnival of the Animals (Video Artists International)
Charlotte's Web
The Cricket in Times Square (3 titles)
The Devil and Daniel Mouse
Digging Up Dinosaurs
Dinosaur!
Dinosaurs!
Doctor De Soto and Other Stories
The Elephant's Child
Funny Stories
Gift of the Whales
The Golden Seal
Great America Series (VideoTours)
Great Events Video Library Series
Gregory and the Terrible Eater/ Gila Monsters Meet You at the Airport
Happy Birthday, Moon and Other Stories
How the Leopard Got His Spots

*How the Rhinoceros Got His Skin/
  How the Camel Got His Hump*
Humphrey the Lost Whale
The Incredible Journey
The Jungle Book (Disney)
The Jungle Book (Embassy)
Lassie Come Home
A Link with Nature
**Lorne Greene's New Wilderness
  Series**
Lyle, Lyle Crocodile: The Musical
Maia: A Dinosaur Grows Up
Medicine Hat Stallion
More Dinosaurs
Morris Goes to School
Mowgli's Brothers
My Family and Other Animals
*The Mysterious Tadpole and
  Other Stories*
National Geographic Series
National Velvet
Never Cry Wolf
Newton's Apple
Noah's Ark
Ocean Symphony
Old Yeller
Owl Moon and Other Stories
The Reluctant Dragon
Rikki-Tikki-Tavi
Rudyard Kipling's Classic Stories
Rudyard Kipling's Just So Stories
*Samson and Sally: The Song of the
  Whales*
**Scholastic Blue Ribbon
  Storybook Video Series**
The Secret of NIMH
The Silent One
Sometimes I Wonder
Strega Nonna and Other Stories
*The Tale of Mr. Jeremy Fisher and
  The Tale of Peter Rabbit*
Tales of Beatrix Potter (ballet)
Tell Me Why Series
*The Three Billy Goats Gruff/
  The Three Little Pigs*
The Three Robbers and Other Stories

*3-2-1 Contact Greatest Hits: Animal
  Tracks*
**The Undersea World of Jacques
  Cousteau Series**
The Very Merry Cricket
Watership Down
When the Whales Came
Where in the World Series
The White Seal
The Wind in the Willows (4 tapes)
A World Alive
Yankee Doodle Cricket
The Yearling

ANIMATION

ABC (Dr. Seuss)
Abel's Island
Alice in Wonderland
The Amazing Bone and Other Stories
An American Tail
Animal Stories
Animated Haggadah
Babar titles
**Bank Street Read-Along Story
  Videos Series**
*BBC Language Course: Muzzy
  French*
*BBC Language Course: Muzzy
  Spanish*
Beauty and the Beast
*Bugs and Daffy's Carnival of the
  Animals*
The Butter Battle Book (Dr. Seuss)
Castle
The Cat in the Hat (Dr. Seuss)
The Cat in the Hat Comes Back (Dr.
  Seuss)
Cathedral
Charlotte's Web
Christmas Stories
Classic Fairy Tales
Clifford's Fun Series
Corduroy and Other Bear Stories
The Cricket in Times Square
*Cricket's Clubhouse: Around the
  World with Cricket*

146 Suggested Video Titles

Dark Crystal
The Devil and Daniel Mouse
Dinosaurs!
Doctor De Soto and Other Stories
Dr. Seuss
Dr. Seuss Festival (Dr. Seuss)
Dr. Seuss on the Loose (Dr. Seuss)
The Elephant's Child
Fables of Harry Allard
First Christmas
The Fisherman and His Wife
Five Lionni Classics
Five Stories for the Very Young
Fun in a Box One
Fun in a Box Two
Funny Stories
The Grinch Grinches Cat in the Hat/Pontoffel Pock (Dr. Seuss)
Goggles
Gregory and the Terrible Eater/ Gila Monsters Meet You at the Airport
Halloween Is Grinch Night (Dr. Seuss)
Happy Birthday, Moon and Other Stories
Homer Price Stories
The Hoober-Bloob Highway (Dr. Seuss)
Hop on Pop (Dr. Seuss)
Horton Hears a Who/The Grinch Who Stole Christmas (Dr. Seuss)
How the Leopard Got His Spots
How the Rhinoceros Got His Skin/How the Camel Got His Hump
Hubley Studio Animation Series
The Human Race Club Series
Jack and the Beanstalk
Joe Scruggs: Joe's First Video
The Jungle Book (Disney)
The Legend of Sleepy Hollow
The Light Princess
Lights
The Lion, the Witch, and the Wardrobe

The Little Match Girl
The Lorax (Dr. Seuss)
Lyle, Lyle Crocodile: The Musical
Madeline: The Musical
Madeline's Rescue
Maia: A Dinosaur Grows Up
The Maurice Sendak Library
Merlin and the Dragons
Mike Mulligan and His Steam Shovel and Other Stories: Also includes "Burt Dow: Deep-Water Man," "Moon Man"
Morris Goes to School
Mowgli's Brothers
The Mysterious Tadpole and Other Stories
National Film Board of Canada Series
Noah's Ark
Norman the Doorman and Other Stories
Nursery Rhymes
One Fish Two Fish Red Fish Blue Fish (Dr. Seuss)
Owl Moon and Other Stories
Paul Bunyan
Pecos Bill
Pegasus
The Point
Pyramid
Really Rosie
Red Riding Hood and Goldilocks
The Red Shoes
The Reluctant Dragon
Richard Scarry's Best Alphabet Video Ever
Richard Scarry's Best Counting Video Ever
Richard Scarry's Tales
Rikki-Tikki-Tavi
The Robert McCloskey Library
Rub a Dub Dub
Rudyard Kipling's Classic Stories
Sadako and the Thousand Paper Cranes

Samson and Sally: The Song of the Whales
Sarah and the Squirrel
Science/Nature Collection
  VideoTours Series
The Secret of NIMH
Smile for Auntie and Other Stories
The Snowman
Steadfast Tin Soldier
The Story about Ping and Other Stories
The Story of the Dancing Frog
Strega Nonna and Other Stories
The Tailor of Gloucester
The Tale of Mr. Jeremy Fisher and The Tale of Peter Rabbit
The Talking Parcels
Teeny-Tiny and the Witch-Woman and Other Scary Stories
The Three Billy Goats Gruff/ The Three Little Pigs
The Three Robbers and Other Stories
3-2-1 Contact Greatest Hits: Animal Tracks
Thumbelina (RCA/Columbia)
Thumbelina (SVS)
The Tin Soldier
Twelve Months
The Ugly Duckling
The Ugly Duckling and Other Classic Fairytales
The Velveteen Rabbit (Family Home Entertainment)
The Velveteen Rabbit (Random House)
The Velveteen Rabbit (Running Press)
The Very Merry Cricket
Watership Down
What's a Good Story? Beauty and the Beast
What's Happening To Me?
What's Under My Bed and Other Creepy Stories
Where Did I Come From?

The White Seal
Yankee Doodle Cricket

BIOGRAPHY

Abe Lincoln: Freedom Fighter
As the Wind Rocks the Wagon
The Author's Eye Series
Booker
The Diary of Anne Frank
Gandhi
Great Events Video Library Series
The Harlem Globetrotters
Island of the Blue Dolphins
Little Women
Man of the Trees
The Miracle Worker
My Family and Other Animals
Thomas Edison: The Boy Who Lit Up the World
Timeline Series
Wilbur and Orville: First To Fly
Will Rogers: Champion of the People
The World of Anne Frank

COMING OF AGE

The Adventures of Huckleberry Finn
Beauty and the Beast
The Boy Who Could Fly
David Copperfield
Eyes of Amaryllis
Gift of the Whales
A Girl of the Limberlost
Hiroshima Maiden
Jacob Have I Loved
The Journey of Natty Gann
Lantern Hill
Looking for Miracles
Medicine Hat Stallion
The Mighty Pawns
Runaway
Starlight Hotel
Sweet 15
When the Whales Came

148 Suggested Video Titles

Where the Red Fern Grows
Who Has Seen the Wind?
The Wild Pony
The Yearling

ENVIRONMENT

Animal ABCs
Animal Wonders from Down Under Series
Animal Zoop, Vol. 2 Series
Animals in Action Series
Armchair Safaris Series
Banana, Banana, Banana Slug
The Blue Frontier Series
The Butter Battle Book
Eco, You and Simon, Too!
Get Ready, Get Set, Grow!
Gift of the Whales
A Girl of the Limberlost
The Golden Seal
Great America Series (VideoTours)
Great Events Video Library Series
Humphrey the Lost Whale
Island of the Blue Dolphins
Let's Be Friends: Tickle Tune Typhoon
A Link with Nature
The Lorax
Lorne Greene's New Wilderness Series
Man of the Trees
My Family and Other Animals
Never Cry Wolf
Samson and Sally: The Song of the Whales
Science/Nature Collection (VideoTours)
3-2-1 Contact Extra Series
The Undersea World of Jacques Cousteau Series
When the Whales Came
Where in the World Series
A World Alive

FAIRY TALES & LEGENDS

The Adventures of Robin Hood
Amahl and the Night Visitors (opera)
American Storytelling Stories Series
An American Tail
Ashpet: An American Cinderella
Babar titles
Bach and Broccoli
Beauty and the Beast (Hi-Tops)
Beauty and the Beast (Nelson)
Cinderella: Rodgers and Hammerstein
Classic Fairy Tales
Dark Crystal
Fables of Harry Allard
Family Circle Presents Storyland Theatre (Vols. 1–6)
The Fisherman and His Wife
Frog
The Frog King
Hansel and Gretel
Hansel and Gretel (opera)
Hansel and Gretel (puppets)
How the Leopard Got His Spots
How the Rhinoceros Got His Skin/How the Camel Got His Hump
Jack and the Beanstalk
Jack and the Dentist's Daughter
The Legend of Sleepy Hollow
The Little Match Girl
The Man Who Didn't Wash for Seven Years
Merlin and the Dragons
Mowgli's Brothers
The Nutcracker: A Fantasy on Ice
The Nutcracker: The Motion Picture (ballet)
Paul Bunyan
Pecos Bill
Pegasus
Red Riding Hood and Goldilocks
Rudyard Kipling's Classic Stories

Rudyard Kipling's Just So Stories
Rumplestiltskin
**Scholastic Blue Ribbon
   Storybook Video** Series
Sleeping Beauty on Ice
Soldier Jack
Steadfast Tin Soldier
Stories and Fables (19 titles)
Sword in the Stone
The Tailor of Gloucester
Tall Tales and Legends Series
*The Three Billy Goats Gruff/
   The Three Little Pigs*
Thumbelina
The Tin Soldier
Tom Thumb
Twelve Months
The Ugly Duckling
*The Ugly Duckling and Other
   Classic Fairytales:* Also
   includes "The Stonecutter,"
   "The Swineherd"
The White Seal

FAMILY

Anne of Avonlea
Anne of Green Gables
Babar titles
The Boy Who Could Fly
The Bridge to Terabithia
A Child's Christmas in Wales
A Christmas Carol
The Electric Grandmother
A Girl of the Limberlost
Hey, What About Me?
The Hideaways
Hiroshima Maiden
Hockey Night
The Human Race Club Series
Jacob Have I Loved
The Journey of Natty Gann
Lantern Hill
Lassie Come Home
Let's Get a Move On
Little Lord Fauntleroy
Little Women

Looking for Miracles
Miracle Down Under
The Miracle Worker
Molly's Pilgrim
My Family and Other Animals
Mystery Island
National Velvet
Necessary Parties
Out of Time
Pollyanna
The Secret Garden
The Secret of NIMH
Sometimes I Wonder
Sweet 15
Swiss Family Robinson
To Kill a Mockingbird
A Tree Grows in Brooklyn
Tuck Everlasting
The Video Letter from Japan Series
A Waltz through the Hills
Where the Red Fern Grows
The Witches
The World of Anne Frank
The Yearling

FANTASY (8 & UP)

The Boy Who Could Fly
The Brothers Lionheart
Buster's World
The Electric Grandmother
Eyes of Amaryllis
The Fisherman and His Wife
Mystery Island
The NeverEnding Story
The Princess Bride
Tuck Everlasting
Watership Down
The Witches

FINE ARTS

Amahl and the Night Visitors
   (opera)
Ballet for Beginners
Carnival of the Animals
   (Twin Tower)

150 Suggested Video Titles

Carnival of the Animals
  (Video Artists International)
Castle
Cathedral
The Children of Theatre Street
A Christmas Carol
Don't Eat the Pictures
Great Events Video Library
  Series
Hansel and Gretel (opera)
The Hideaways
Higglety Pigglety Pop! (opera)
Hubley Studio Animation Series
I Can Dance
Maestro's Company, Vol. 1 (opera)
Maestro's Company, Vol. 2 (opera)
National Film Board of Canada
  Series
The Nutcracker: A Fantasy on Ice
The Nutcracker: The Motion Picture
  (ballet)
Pyramid
Sleeping Beauty on Ice
Tales of Beatrix Potter (ballet)
Teach Me To Dance
Who's Afraid of Opera?

HISTORY

Abe Lincoln: Freedom Fighter
The Adventures of Huckleberry Finn
The Adventures of Robin Hood
Amahl and the Night Visitors
  (opera)
An American Tail
And the Children Shall Lead
Animated Haggadah
As the Wind Rocks the Wagon
The Autobiography of Miss Jane
  Pittman
Booker
Captains Courageous
Castle
Cathedral
A Connecticut Yankee at King
  Arthur's Court
David Copperfield
The Diary of Anne Frank
Eyes of Amaryllis
Gandhi
Great America Series
  (VideoTours)
Great Events Video Library
  Series
Hiroshima Maiden
History Collection (VideoTours)
Island of the Blue Dolphins
Ivanhoe
John and Julie
The Journey of Natty Gann
Kids Ask about War
Kim
Lift Off
Lights
Little Lord Fauntleroy
The Little Princess (Public Media
  Video)
Little Women
Looking for Miracles
Maia: A Dinosaur Grows Up
Medicine Hat Stallion
Miracle at Moreaux
The Miracle Worker
Molly's Pilgrim
Noah's Ark
Oliver!
Oliver Twist
Out of Time
Pyramid
Sadako and the Thousand Paper
  Cranes
Sarah and the Squirrel
Sounder
Tell Me Why Series
Thomas Edison: The Boy Who Lit
  Up the World
Timeline Series
To Kill a Mockingbird
The Tortoise and the Hare and Hill
  of Fire
Treasure Island
A Tree Grows in Brooklyn

Who Has Seen the Wind?
Wilbur and Orville: First To Fly
Will Rogers: Champion of the People
The World of Anne Frank
Yankee Doodle Cricket

LANGUAGE ARTS

ABC (Dr. Seuss)
Abel's Island
The Adventures of Huckleberry Finn
Alice in Wonderland
Amahl and the Night Visitors (opera)
The Amazing Bone and Other Stories
American Storytelling Stories Series
Animal ABCs
Animal Alphabet Series
Animal Stories
Ashpet: An American Cinderella
The Author's Eye Series
The Autobiography of Miss Jane Pittman
Babar titles
Banana, Banana, Banana Slug
Bank Street Read-Along Story Videos Series
Barney and the Backyard Gang: Barney Goes to School
Beauty and the Beast (Hi-Tops)
Beauty and the Beast (Nelson)
Big Bird in China
The Box of Delights
The Bridge to Terabithia
Buster's World
The Butter Battle Book (Dr. Seuss)
Captains Courageous
Castle
The Cat in the Hat (Dr. Seuss)
The Cat in the Hat Comes Back (Dr. Seuss)
Cathedral
Charlie Chaplin Series
Charlotte's Web
A Christmas Carol

Christmas Stories
A Connecticut Yankee at King Arthur's Court
Corduroy and Other Bear Stories
The Cricket in Times Square
David Copperfield
Doctor De Soto and Other Stories
Dr. Seuss
Dr. Seuss Festival (Dr. Seuss)
Dr. Seuss on the Loose (Dr. Seuss)
Eco, You and Simon, Too!
The Electric Grandmother
The Elephant's Child
Fables of Harry Allard
Family Circle Presents Storyland Theatre
The Fisherman and His Wife
Five Stories for the Very Young
The Frog King
Funny Stories
Great Events Video Library Series
Gregory and the Terrible Eater/Gila Monsters Meet You at the Airport
The Grinch Grinches Cat in the Hat/Pontoffel Pock (Dr. Seuss)
Halloween Is Grinch Night (Dr. Seuss)
Hansel and Gretel
Happy Birthday, Moon and Other Stories
The Hideaways
Homer Price Stories
The Hoober-Bloob Highway (Dr. Seuss)
Hop on Pop (Dr. Seuss)
Horton Hears a Who/The Grinch Who Stole Christmas (Dr. Seuss)
How the Leopard Got His Spots
How the Rhinoceros Got His Skin/How the Camel Got His Hump
How To Be a Perfect Person in Just Three Days
Island of the Blue Dolphins
Ivanhoe

152 Suggested Video Titles

Jack and the Dentist's Daughter
The Jungle Book (Disney)
The Jungle Book (Embassy)
Kids in Action
Kim
Lantern Hill
The Legend of Sleepy Hollow
The Light Princess
The Lion, the Witch and the Wardrobe
The Little Match Girl
The Little Princess (Active, Playhouse)
The Little Princess (Public Media Video)
Little Women
Looking for Miracles
The Lorax (Dr. Seuss)
Macmillan Video Almanac for Kids Series
Madeline: The Musical
Madeline's Rescue
The Man Who Didn't Wash for Seven Years
The Maurice Sendak Library
Merlin and the Dragons
Mike Mulligan and His Steam Shovel and Other Stories
Morris Goes to School
Mowgli's Brothers
The Mysterious Tadpole and Other Stories
National Film Board of Canada Series
The NeverEnding Story
Noah's Ark
Norman the Doorman and Other Stories
Nursery Rhymes
Oliver Twist
One Fish Two Fish Red Fish Blue Fish (Dr. Seuss)
Owl Moon and Other Stories
Paul Bunyan
Pecos Bill
Pegasus

Pippi Longstocking Series
Pyramid
Red Riding Hood and Goldilocks
Richard Scarry's Best Alphabet Video Ever
Richard Scarry's Tales
Rikki-Tikki-Tavi
Rub a Dub Dub
Rudyard Kipling's Classic Stories
Rudyard Kipling's Just So Stories
Rumplestiltskin
Runaway
Runaway Island Series
Sadako and the Thousand Paper Cranes
Say It by Signing
Scholastic Blue Ribbon Storybook Video Series
The Secret Garden
Shirley Temple Series
Sign Me a Story
Silent Mouse
Sleeping Beauty on Ice
Smile for Auntie and Other Stories
The Snowman
Soldier Jack
Stories and Fables
The Story about Ping and Other Stories
Strega Nonna and Other Stories
Swiss Family Robinson
Sword in the Stone
The Tailor of Gloucester
The Tale of Mrs. Jeremy Fisher and the Tale of Peter Rabbit
Tall Tales and Legends Series
Teeny-Tiny and the Witch-Woman and Other Scary Stories
The Three Billy Goats Gruff/ The Three Little Pigs
The Three Musketeers
The Three Robbers and Other Stories
Thumbelina (RCA/Columbia)
Thumbelina (SVS)
To Kill a Mockingbird
Tom Thumb

Treasure Island
A Tree Grows in Brooklyn
The Ugly Duckling
The Ugly Duckling and Other Classic Fairytales
The Velveteen Rabbit (Family Home Entertainment)
The Velveteen Rabbit (Random House)
The Velveteen Rabbit (Running Press)
What's a Good Story? Beauty and the Beast
What's Under My Bed and Other Creepy Stories
Where the Red Fern Grows
The White Seal
The Yearling

MULTICULTURE

The Adventures of Huckleberry Finn
Amahl and the Night Visitors (opera)
An American Tail
And the Children Shall Lead
Animated Haggadah
Arthur's Eyes
Ashpet: An American Cinderella
The Autobiography of Miss Jane Pittman
BBC Language Course: Muzzy French
BBC Language Course: Muzzy Spanish
Big Bird in China
Booker
Chanuka at Bubbe's
The Children of Theatre Street
A Child's Christmas in Wales
The Diary of Anne Frank
Discover Korea
Gandhi
Gift of the Whales
Goggles
Great Events Video Library Series

Hansel and Gretel
Hiroshima Maiden
Hubley Studio Animation Series
Island of the Blue Dolphins
John and Julie
The Jungle Book (Disney)
The Jungle Book (Embassy)
Kids Ask about War
Kim
The Little Match Girl
Macmillan Video Almanac for Kids Series
Man of the Trees
Medicine Hat Stallion
The Mighty Pawns
Miracle at Moreaux
Molly's Pilgrim
My Family and Other Animals
Pippi Longstocking Series
The Red Shoes
Run, Rebecca, Run!
Sadako and the Thousand Paper Cranes
Shalom Sesame Series
Silent Mouse
The Silent One
Sounder
Stories of American Indian Culture Series
Sweet 15
Teach Me To Dance
Timeline Series
To Kill a Mockingbird
The Video Letter from Japan Series
A Waltz through the Hills
When the Whales Came

MUSIC

Alice in Wonderland
Amahl and the Night Visitors (opera)
Animal Alphabet Series
Baboons, Butterflies and Me
Ballet for Beginners

154 Suggested Video Titles

Barney and the Backyard Gang:
    Barney Goes to School
Bugs and Daffy's Carnival of the
    Animals
Carnival of the Animals
    (Twin Tower)
Carnival of the Animals
    (Video Artists International)
Chanuka at Bubbe's
Charlotte's Web
The Children of Theatre Street
Cinderella: Rodgers and
    Hammerstein
Eco, You and Simon, Too!
**Great Events Video Library
    Series**
Hansel and Gretel (opera)
Higglety Pigglety Pop! (opera)
I Can Dance
Jack and the Beanstalk
**Jim Henson's Play-Along Video
    Series**
Joe Scruggs: Joe's First Video
Kids in Action
Kidsongs Series
Let's Be Friends: Tickle Tune
    Typhoon
A Link with Nature
Lyle, Lyle Crocodile: The Musical
Madeline: The Musical
Maestro's Company, Vol. 1 (opera)
Maestro's Company, Vol. 2 (opera)
The Maurice Sendak Library
The Nutcracker: A Fantasy on Ice
The Nutcracker: The Motion Picture
    (ballet)
Oliver!
The Point
Really Rosie
The Red Shoes
Silent Mouse
Sleeping Beauty on Ice
The Story of the Dancing Frog
Tales of Beatrix Potter (ballet)
3-2-1 Contact Greatest Hits: Animal
    Tracks

Tom Thumb
Where the Wild Things Are (opera)
Who's Afraid of Opera?
The Wizard of Oz

REFERENCE

**American Storytelling Stories
    Series**
Animal ABCs
**Animal Wonders from Down
    Under Series
Animal Zoop, Vol. 2 Series
Animals in Action Series**
Animals of Africa
Animated Haggadah
Armchair Safaris Series
As the Wind Rocks the Wagon
The Author's Eye Series
BBC Language Course: Muzzy
    French
BBC Language Course: Muzzy
    Spanish
Be a Juggler
Be a Magician
Buy Me That!
Castle
Cathedral
Chanuka at Bubbe's
Choosing the Best in Children's
    Video
The Dream Is Alive
From Star Wars to Jedi: The Making
    of a Saga
Get Ready, Get Set, Grow!
**Great America Series
    (VideoTours)
Great Events Video Library
    Series**
The Harlem Globetrotters
Here We Go (Vols. 1–2)
Herschel Walker's Fitness
    Challenges for Kids
Hey, What about Me
History Collection (VideoTours)
Home Alone

How To Draw Comics the Marvel Way
I Can Dance
Inside the Labyrinth
Jim Henson's Play-Along Video Series
Kids Ask about War
Kids for Safety
Kids in Action
Let's Get a Move On
Lift Off!
Lights
Little League's Official How-To-Play Baseball by Video
Look What I Made: Paper Playthings and Gifts
Lorne Greene's New Wilderness Series
Macmillan Video Almanac for Kids Series
National Geographic Series
Newton's Apple
Ocean Symphony
1-2-3 Magic Series
Pyramid
Sadako and the Thousand Paper Cranes
Say It by Signing
Science/Nature Collection (VideoTours)
Shalom Sesame Series
Sign Me a Story
Squiggles, Dots and Lines
Tell Me Why Series
3-2-1 Contact Extra Series
Timeline Series
Video Flash Cards (8 titles)
The Video Guide to Stamp Collecting
The Video Letter from Japan Series
What's Happening To Me?
Where Did I Come From?
Where in the World Series
Who's Afraid of Opera?
A World Alive
The World of Anne Frank
You Can Choose Series

SCIENCE

Animal ABCs
Animal Wonders from Down Under Series
Animal Zoop, Vol. 2 Series
Animals in Action Series
Banana, Banana, Banana Slug
The Blue Frontier Series
The Butter Battle Book (Dr. Seuss)
Digging Up Dinosaurs
Dinosaur!
Dinosaurs!
Dr. Seuss
The Dream Is Alive
Get Ready, Get Set, Grow!
Gift of the Whales
Great America Series (VideoTours)
Great Events Video Library Series
Humphrey the Lost Whale
Lift Off!
Lorne Greene's New Wilderness Series
Macmillan Video Almanac for Kids Series
Maia: A Dinosaur Grows Up
More Dinosaurs
National Geographic Series
Newton's Apple
Ocean Symphony
Science/Nature Collection (VideoTours)
Tell Me Why Series
3-2-1 Contact Extra Series
The Undersea World of Jacques Cousteau Series
Walking on Air
What's Happening To Me?
Where Did I Come From?
A World Alive

TRAVEL

The Adventures of Milo and Otis
Animal Wonders from Down Under

156 Suggested Video Titles

Animals of Africa
Armchair Safaris Series
Big Bird in China
The Black Stallion
The Black Stallion Returns
The Blue Frontier Series
Born Free
The Children of Theatre Street
A Child's Christmas in Wales
Cricket's Clubhouse: Around the World with Cricket
Discover Korea
The Dream Is Alive
The Flight of the Navigator
Great America Series (VideoTours)
Gregory and the Terrible Eater/Gila Monsters Meet You at the Airport
Here We Go (Vols. 1–2)
History Collection (VideoTours)
The Incredible Journey
Kidsongs Series
Lift Off!
Madeline: The Musical
Maestro's Company, Vol. 1 (opera)
Maestro's Company, Vol. 2 (opera)
Man of the Trees
Miracle Down Under
My Family and Other Animals
Pippi Longstocking Series
Run, Rebecca, Run!
Science/Nature Collection (VideoTours)
Shalom Sesame Series
Silent Mouse
The Silent One
Timeline Series
Tommy Tricker and the Stamp Traveller
The Video Letter from Japan Series
Where in the World Series
The Young Magician

VIDEO SERIES

Children's Circle/CC Studios
The Amazing Bone and Other Stories
Animal Stories
Christmas Stories
Corduroy and Other Bear Stories
Doctor De Soto and Other Stories
Five Stories for the Very Young
Funny Stories
Happy Birthday, Moon and Other Stories
Homer Price Stories
Madeline's Rescue
The Maurice Sendak Library
Mike Mulligan and His Steam Shovel and Other Stories
The Mysterious Tadpole and Other Stories
Norman the Doorman and Other Stories
Owl Moon and Other Stories
The Robert McCloskey Library
Smile for Auntie and Other Stories
The Snowman
The Story about Ping and Other Stories
Strega Nonna and Other Stories
Teeny-Tiny and the Witch-Woman and Other Scary Stories
The Three Robbers and Other Stories
The Ugly Duckling and Other Classic Fairytales
What's Under My Bed and Other Creepy Stories
From the Brothers Grimm
Ashpet: An American Cinderella
The Frog King
Hansel and Gretel
Jack and the Dentist's Daughter
The Man Who Didn't Wash for Seven Years
Soldier Jack
Rabbit Ears Productions
The Elephant's Child
The Fisherman and His Wife
How the Leopard Got His Spots

*How the Rhinoceros Got His
    Skin/How the Camel Got
    His Hump*
The Legend of Sleepy Hollow
Paul Bunyan
Pecos Bill
Red Riding Hood and Goldilocks
The Tailor of Gloucester
*The Tale of Mr. Jeremy Fisher and
    The Tale of Peter Rabbit*
*The Three Billy Goats Gruff/
    The Three Little Pigs*
Thumbelina
The Ugly Duckling
The Velveteen Rabbit
Reading Rainbow
*Gregory and the Terrible Eater/
    Gila Monsters Meet You at
    the Airport*
Humphrey the Lost Whale
*The Tortoise and the Hare
    and Hill of Fire*
Stories To Remember
Beauty and the Beast
Merlin and the Dragons
Noah's Ark
Pegasus
WonderWorks
And the Children Shall Lead

Anne of Avonlea
Anne of Green Gables
Booker
The Box of Delights
The Bridge to Terabithia
Buster's World
Frog
A Girl of the Limberlost
Hiroshima Maiden
Hockey Night
*How To Be a Perfect Person
    in Just Three Days*
Jacob Have I Loved
Lantern Hill
*The Little Princess
    (Public Media Video)*
Looking for Miracles
The Mighty Pawns
Miracle at Moreaux
Miracle Down Under
Necessary Parties
Runaway
Run, Rebecca, Run!
The Silent One
Sweet 15
Walking on Air
A Waltz through the Hills
Who Has Seen the Wind?
The Wild Pony

APPENDIX B

Organizations

KidsNet
6856 Eastern Avenue, NW
Suite 208
Washington, DC 20012
(202) 291-1400
  KidsNet is a national clearinghouse for children's TV and radio. *Future Bulletin and Calendar* is available as part of a KidsNet subscription, or as a separate monthly subscription.

National Captioning Institute, Inc.
5203 Leesburg Pike, 15th Floor
Falls Church, VA 22041
(800) 533-WORD (voice);
(800) 321-TDDS (TDD)
  NCI is the manufacturer of Tele-Caption 4000, a closed-caption decoder. The company also creates closed captioning for videos. Write or call for list of captioned videos.

National Telemedia Council, Inc.
120 East Wilson Street
Madison, WI 53703
(608) 257-7712
  National Telemedia Council, Inc., is dedicated to the belief that children can be in control of rather than under the control of television. Members receive the quarterly newsletter *Telemedium, Telemedium Update,* and other mailings, plus invitations to and reduced rates for conferences and workshops. Educational materials and curriculum aids and the *Annual Look/Listen Report* are free on request.

Strategies for Media Literacy, Inc.
347 Dolores Street, Room 306
San Francisco, CA 94110
(415) 621-2911
  SML is an organization that promotes media studies across the curriculum beginning in early elementary school. The organization develops and publishes, identifies, and serves as a center of support and contact for teachers of media, and publishes a quarterly newsletter. Write for information.

The following organizations provide programs for instructing children in the use of media:

Children's Media Lab
P.O. Box 9237
Berkeley, CA 94709-0237
(415) 223-6528

Educational Video Center, Inc.
60 East 13th Street, 4th Floor
New York, NY 10003
(212) 254-2848

160 Organizations

Project Six Foundation, Inc.
P.O. Box 9413
San Rafael, CA 94912-1807
(415) 459-1807

Rise and Shine Productions
1600 Broadway, Room 610
New York, NY 10019
(212) 265-0359

Video Resources Studio
Norman Public Schools
911 West Main Street
Norman, OK 73069
(405) 366-5821

Distributors of Children's Video

A number of distributors offer discounts to schools and libraries. Call or write for information on these, as well as on policies regarding previewing, public performance rights, and duplication rights.

Baker and Taylor Video
501 South Gladiolus
Momence, IL 60954
(800) 435-5111;
in Illinois (800) 892-1892
   Produces inexpensive educational home videos. Call or write for the elementary catalog.

Coronet Feature Video
108 Wilmot Road
Deerfield, IL 60015-9925
(800) 621-2131
   Request information on the Public Library Collection.

Facets Video
1517 West Fullerton Avenue
Chicago, IL 60614
(800) 331-6197;
in Illinois (312) 281-9075
   Distributor for videos of foreign and classic films as well as for independently produced videos.

Films Incorporated
5547 North Ravenswood Avenue
Chicago, IL 60640-9976
(800) 323/4222, extension 236;
in Illinois, call collect (312) 878-2600
   Offers four catalogs that include children's programming: *The Films Incorporated Video Catalog for Licensed Public Showings; The Programmer's Index to the Classic Collection; The Comprehensive Index;* and *The Specialty Catalog: American, Foreign and Silent.*

Library Video Company
Department M-3
P.O. Box 40351
Philadelphia, PA 19106
(800) VIDEO-20
   Distributor of educational videos.

Upbeat Video
163 Joralemon Street, Suite 1250
Brooklyn, NY 11201
(800) 872-3288
   Distributes a number of children's titles, including hard-to-find audio and video.

Video Databank
37 South Wabash
Chicago, IL 60603
(312) 899-5172
   Request catalog of videos about media literacy.

The Video Project
5332 College Avenue, Suite 101
Oakland, CA 94618
(415) 655-9050;
call (800) 4-PLANET for the automated ordering line (be ready to cite pertinent information and have a credit card number or purchase order number ready)

    A nonprofit media resource center that distributes educational videos about the environment and other critical global issues.

Zenger Video
10200 Jefferson Boulevard
Room TM
P.O. Box 802
Culver City, CA 90232-0802
(800) 421-4246;
in California (213) 839-2436

    Distributes educational videos, including children's, social studies, literature, home economics, and humanities.

APPENDIX C

Print Resources

Specialty Publications

"Access for Children and Young People to Videotapes and Other Nonprint Formats" and "Freedom To View"
American Library Association
50 East Huron Street
Chicago, IL 60611
(312) 944-6780

California Index of Instructional Video
California Instructional Video
 Clearinghouse
801 County Center Three Court
Modesto, CA 95355
(209) 525-4993

> This two-volume publication rates more than 4,050 film/video programs. Volume 1 ranks the programs by producers and Volume 2 ranks them by subject matter. You might also inquire as to whether your state has such an index.

Using Copyrighted Videocassettes in Classrooms, Libraries and Training Centers, by Jerome Miller

Copyright Information Services
P.O. Box 1460-B
Friday Harbor, WA 98250
(206) 378-5128

> CIS also has several other publications explaining copyright licensing rights for off-air taping.

Books about Literature and Story

Applebee, Arthur. *The Child's Concept of Story: Ages Two to Seventeen.* Chicago: University of Chicago Press, 1978.

> This book focuses on how children respond to and interact with stories, as well as how they use and understand language. Included are summaries of numerous studies and tables that condense and clarify the author's research.

Bettelheim, Bruno. *The Uses of Enchantment: The Meaning and Importance of Fairy Tales.* New York: Vintage, 1977.

In this landmark book, psychologist Bettelheim explores the ways that fairy tales enrich children's lives and analyzes several familiar tales. Although readers may not agree with his premise, they will be stimulated to think through their own beliefs. This volume is a must for anyone thinking about children and fairy tales.

Bottigheimer, Ruth B. *Grimms' Bad Girls and Bad Boys: The Moral and Social Vision of the Tales.* New Haven, CT: Yale University Press, 1987.

In this thoroughly researched, scholarly, and thought-provoking work, Bottigheimer provides a content analysis of Grimms' tales with respect to plot, motif, image, and dialogue. By examining patterns that emerge through overlapping motifs and themes, she draws conclusions about gender distinctions with reference to Christianity, laying spells, speech, and the transformation of power.

Carpenter, Humphrey. *Secret Gardens: The Golden Age of Children's Literature from Alice in Wonderland to Winnie the Pooh.* Boston: Houghton Mifflin, 1985.

Within a span of 70 years, England spawned writers such as Charles Kingsley (*The Water Babies*), Lewis Carroll (*Alice in Wonderland*), George MacDonald (*The Light Princess*), Frances Hodgson (*Little Lord Fauntleroy, The Secret Garden*), Beatrix Potter (*The Tales of Peter Rabbit*), Kenneth Grahame (*The Wind in the Willows, The Reluctant Dragon*), James Matthew Barrie (*Peter Pan*), and Alan Alexander Milne (*Winnie the Pooh*). Carpenter examines the lives and works of these writers and speculates on what they had in common. All of the books mentioned above have been adapted for video.

Coles, Robert. *The Call of Stories: Teaching and the Moral Imagination.* Boston: Houghton Mifflin, 1989.

In this book, Coles examines the long-term effect of story and its importance as a vehicle for moral insights, making references to specific short stories and books and reflecting on his own childhood and the value his family placed on story. Included are excerpts from interviews in which people reveal how their lives and ways of thinking have been shaped by literary characters. Like all of Coles's books, this one provides an opportunity for honest reflection.

Cook, Elizabeth. *The Ordinary and the Fabulous: An Introduction to Myths, Legends and Fairy Tales.* Cambridge, England: Cambridge University Press, 1976.

Cook interprets familiar legends and tales and discusses how they can best be explored with children, particularly those in the often-overlooked 8–14 age range. She then offers an annotated list of children's books, including Greek myths and legends; fairy tales for children under 7 and for children 8 through 11; modern hybrid myths, legends, and fantasies; myths, legends, and fairy tales from the Third World and from Eastern Europe and the Near East; and American Indian and African-American stories. Also included are books on children's books; using stories in the classroom; interpretation of myths, legends, and fairy tales; psychological criticism; and studies of development in literature.

Cott, Jonathan. *Pipers at the Gates of Dawn: The Wisdom of Children's*

Literature. New York: McGraw-Hill, 1981.

> Cott presents a discussion of the work of six writers of children's books: Dr. Seuss, Maurice Sendak, William Steig, Astrid Lindgren, Chinua Achebe, and P. L. Travers. He also reflects on the work of Iona and Peter Opie, the contemporary scholars of children's literature, games, and language. Included is a complete listing of books written and/or illustrated by the featured authors.

Dorfman, Ariel. *The Empire's Old Clothes: What the Lone Ranger, Babar, and Other Innocent Heroes Do to Our Minds.* New York: Pantheon, 1983.

> Dorfman's book is an exploration of the hidden social and political meanings behind the faces seen in many children's books, comics, and magazines. Dorfman provides an interesting point of view that, although readers may disagree with it, will prompt reflection.

Dorfman, Ariel, and A. Mattelart. *How To Read Donald Duck: Imperialist Ideology in the Disney Comic.* New York: International General, 1984.

> In this thought-provoking book, Dorfman and Mattelart, who believe that capitalism and imperialist values are supported by American culture, offer a Marxist analysis of Disney and Disney's creations. In the introduction to the English edition of this book, David Kunzle states that "Disney is no conjuror," and goes on to say that the authors "expose the magician's sleight of hand, to reveal the scowl of capitalist ideology behind the laughing mask, the iron fist beneath the Mouse's glove."

Dundes, Alan, editor. *Cinderella: A Casebook.* Madison: University of Wisconsin Press, 1988.

> The essays included in this fascinating book were written over the last 100 years; they espouse a variety of viewpoints and explore several versions of the fairy tale. Included is Dundes's own "To Love My Father All: A Psychoanalytic Study of the Folktale Source of King Lear," along with Paul Delarue's "From Perrault to Walt Disney: The Slipper of Cinderella," R. D. Jameson's "Cinderella in China," William Bascom's "Cinderella in Africa," Jane Yolen's "America's Cinderella," and 14 others.

Egoff, Sheila, G. T. Stubbs, and L. F. Ashley, editors. *Only Connect: Readings on Children's Literature* (2nd ed.). Toronto: Oxford University Press, 1980.

> This is a book of literate essays by eminent writers for both children and adults, among them P. L. Travers, C. S. Lewis, J. R. R. Tolkien, Elizabeth Janeway, Graham Greene, and T. S. Eliot. Many of the works mentioned have been adapted to film or video.

Lipson, Eden Ross. *The New York Times Parent's Guide to the Best Books for Children.* New York: Random House, 1988.

> This useful guide includes summaries of hundreds of children's books, divided into sections such as "wordless books," "picture books," and "middle reading books." In most cases the title is accompanied by a one- or two-sentence description, with longer summaries for longer books. Included are author, illustrator, and title indexes, as well as an excellent special subject index.

Opie, Iona, and Peter Opie. *The Classic Fairy Tales*. New York: Oxford University Press, 1974.

> This book contains the original texts of 24 fairy tales. Each story includes an introduction featuring interesting historical background information.

Oppenheim, Joanne, et al. *Choosing Books for Kids: How To Choose the Right Book for the Right Child at the Right Time*. New York: Ballantine, 1986.

> This useful guidebook features reviews of more than 1,500 books written for babies through 12-year-olds. Included are year-by-year descriptions of child development, along with books that work well with each age.

Pearson, Carol S. *The Hero Within: Six Archetypes We Live By*. New York: Harper & Row, 1986.

> Although not explicitly about literature or video, this book is useful for understanding the ramifications of a "hero's journey" in general and specifically how the journey relates to children's understanding of a hero.

Polette, Nancy, and Marjorie Hamlin. *Exploring Books with Gifted Children*. Littleton, CO: Libraries Unlimited, 1980.

> This excellent book offers hundreds of reasons to find good books for children to read and myriad ideas for challenging young minds and enriching reading programs. Many of the books discussed have been adapted to video. Also, many of the activities described for use with specific books may be adapted to other stories and/or other media, including video. Despite the title, the information and ideas in the book are applicable to children of all abilities.

Rudman, Masha Kabakow. *Children's Literature: An Issues Approach* (2nd ed.). New York: Longman, 1984.

> Eight of the ten chapters in this book explore children's literature as it relates to different life issues: the family, sex, gender roles, heritage, special needs, old age, death, and war. Each chapter begins with a general discussion of the topic, followed by related activities to use with children. Also included in each chapter are an annotated list of selected relevant books and a listing of additional resources with addresses. The activities alone make this book a worthwhile resource for anyone using video with children. Also useful are the listings in Appendix B of awards for children's books, many of which have been adapted to video.

Rudman, Masha Kabakow, Anna Markus Pearce, and the Editors of Consumer Reports Books. *For Love of Reading: A Parent's Guide to Encouraging Young Readers from Infancy through Age 5*. Mount Vernon, NY: Consumer Reports Books, 1988.

> This book offers many ideas to help parents share a love for the printed word with their children. One chapter, "Taming the One-Eyed Monster," focuses on selected television programs for children, with an eye to using television as "a resource for encouraging children to think, read, and write." The book's only major flaw is the lack of an index.

Sale, Roger. *Fairy Tales and After: From Snow White to E. B. White*. Cambridge, MA: Harvard University Press, 1978.

This clear and provocative critical discussion on children's literature examines fairy tales and stories about animals with human qualities such as the ability to talk (anthropomorphism). Included are discussions of Lewis Carroll's Alice books, Beatrix Potter, Kenneth Grahame, Rudyard Kipling, L. Frank Baum, and what Sale calls the "Two Pigs"—Freddy from Walter R. Brooks's Freddy books and Wilbur from E. B. White's *Charlotte's Web*.

von Franz, Marie-Louise. *Individuation in Fairy Tales* (rev. ed.). Boston: Shambhala, 1990.

The author discusses the theme of transformation, using as a model six fairy tales about a bird. Included are translations of the six tales, which come from Spain, Persia, Turkey, Iran, Albania, and Austria.

Zipes, Jack. *The Brothers Grimm: From Enchanted Forests to the Modern World*. New York: Routledge, 1988.

Zipes discusses the social, political, and personal elements of the lives of the Grimm brothers as an aid to understanding their tales.

Zipes, Jack, editor. *Don't Bet on the Prince: Contemporary Feminist Fairy Tales in North America and England*. New York: Methuen, 1986.

Zipes's lucid introduction gives an overview of the reasons feminist fairy tales fill a large need in the fairy tale genre: "The structure of most of the feminist tales is based on the self-definition of a young woman. The female protagonist becomes aware of a task which she must complete in social interaction with others to define herself." Following this are 20 tales by writers such as Angela Carter, Jane Yolen, Judith Viorst, and two contributions by Zipes himself—a thorough presentation.

Zipes, Jack. *Fairy Tales and the Art of Subversion: The Classical Genre for Children and the Process of Civilization*. New York: Methuen, 1988.

Zipes presents a social history of the fairy tale from the seventeenth through the twentieth centuries, examining the work of storytellers such as Charles Perrault, Jacob and Wilhelm Grimm, Hans Christian Andersen, George MacDonald, Oscar Wilde, and L. Frank Baum. He then goes on to comment on the subversion of fairy tales during the Weimar and Nazi periods in Germany and in the post–World War II West. This is an interesting look at fairy tales and society.

Books about Media

Bilowit, Debbi. *Critical Television Viewing*. New York: Globe, 1980.

As of this writing, WNET/THIRTEEN in New York is revising and updating this work-a-text. The purpose of the 1980 edition is to teach critical viewing skills to students in sixth through eighth grades by utilizing existing curricula. It is not necessary to create additional materials to teach the concepts in the work-a-text, nor do students need to complete the entire book; they will benefit from isolated lessons as well. Teachers of all grades will benefit from this paperback text, which is filled with ideas, vocabulary words, and activities. Also included are a glossary and an annotated bibliography. (Critical Viewing Skills

168 Print Resources

Project, c/o Education Department, WNET/THIRTEEN, 356 West 58th Street, New York, NY 10019.)

Boggs, Joseph M. *The Art of Watching Films.* Palo Alto, CA: Mayfield, 1985.

Written for adults, this book will serve as "Film Appreciation 101" for those not versed in film criticism. Boggs walks the reader through the important elements of a film, giving examples from classics and contemporary movies and using photographs to clarify points. Each chapter is followed by a series of questions covering the salient points discussed. These may serve as models for developing additional questions.

Broadman, Muriel. *Understanding Your Child's Entertainment.* New York: Harper & Row, 1977.

Broadman's understanding of children is based on her extensive knowledge of child development and children's theater. She looks at what children learn from specific types of entertainment, such as theater, television, movies, and puppetry, addressing what they take away from an event and how it affects them once it's over. She asks questions such as, Is the story respectful of its audience? Is it relevant to today's audience? Are there any implications, unintended or otherwise, that are not in the audience's best interest? Broadman presents many examples to substantiate her opinions; this is a thoughtful book with many practical observations.

Brown, Laurene K. *Taking Advantage of the Media: A Manual for Parents and Teachers.* Boston: Routledge & Kegan Paul, 1986.

This thoroughly researched and entertaining book focuses on the impact of story on children and how the way the story is learned (heard, print, TV, or computer) affects a child's understanding of it. There is much practical information here that will benefit anyone working with children.

Brown, Marc, and Laurene Krasny Brown. *The Bionic Bunny.* Boston: Little, Brown, 1984.

This children's book offers a clear explanation of how television programs are created. A glimpse behind the scenes of "The Bionic Bunny" TV program shows the cast, crew, and technicians "making television" to create a truly remarkable superhero.

Bryant, Jennings, and D. R. Anderson, editors. *Children's Understanding of Television: Research on Attention and Comprehension.* New York: Academic Press, 1983.

This textbook examines the major research on what children learn by watching television, including assumptions, methodologies, theories, and major findings. In addition to the editors, some of the contributors include Althea Huston and John Wright, Gavriel Salomon, Keith W. Mielke, and Jerome and Dorothy Singer. Of particular interest to producers will be Robert Krull's chapter, "Children Learning To Watch Television." Also included are recommendations based on research findings on how and what children learn from television.

Canemaker, John, editor. *Storytelling in Animation.* Los Angeles: American Film Institute, 1988.

This anthology includes 13 articles and conversations with leading animators and critics of animation. Included are observations and comments written by former Disney employees. Of particular interest is the article by Charles Solomon, who describes the differences between Saturday-morning fare and artful animation. (The American Film Institute, Educational Services, P.O. Box 27999, 2021 North Western Avenue, Los Angeles, CA 90027.)

Comstock, George, et al. *Television and Human Behavior*. New York: Columbia University Press, 1978.

The social and behavioral effects of television viewing are examined by some of the primary researchers of television. The book also includes an extensive reference list that will prove useful for readers involved in current research.

Gaffney, Maureen. *Using Media To Make Kids Feel Good: Resources and Activities for Successful Programs in Hospitals*. Phoenix, AZ: Oryx, 1988.

Although written for people using media in a hospital setting, this book would be useful for anyone using short films with young children. Gaffney provides thorough annotations of the suggested films, including a critical analysis of the quality of each program's content and production, as well as recommended age ranges.

Gaffney, Maureen, and G. Laybourne. *What To Do When the Lights Go On: A Comprehensive Guide to 16mm Films and Related Activities for Children*. Phoenix, AZ: Oryx, 1981.

This sourcebook is filled with ideas to help educators use media creatively with children. Film programs with specific titles are noted, and the overall objective of each program is clearly stated. Many art activities (called "recipes") are offered, along with necessary materials. An annotated listing of films that have been thoroughly researched with children is included. The thorough index makes the book a pleasure to use.

Gallant, Jennifer Jung. *Best Videos for Children and Young Adults: A Core Collection for Libraries*. Santa Barbara, CA: ABC-CLIO, 1990.

This is an annotated listing of approximately 350 notable VHS video titles that may be used with children in kindergarten through twelfth grade. Each citation includes target age audience (preschool, primary, intermediate, junior high, high school), usage (classroom, discussion, recreation), production information (date, color/black and white, sound time, VHS price, with public performance rights and/or home use), director, producer, and distributor. The book also includes a listing of video distributors and useful resources.

Gitlin, Todd, editor. *Watching Television*. New York: Pantheon, 1986.

In addition to discussions on the news, soap operas, music videos, and prime-time television, this book features a chapter on children's television in which Tom Engelhardt comments on the 30-minute commercials for "Care Bears," "HeMan," and "Strawberry Shortcake."

Green, Diana Huss, editor. *Guide to VideoCassettes for Children*. New York: Consumer Reports Books, 1989.

Green is the editor of *Parents Choice*, a quarterly that reviews children's media. She coordinated journalists to review more than 300 titles of videos that children will enjoy.

Following each review are the titles of two books that will complement the video.

Greenfield, Patricia Marks. *Mind and Media: The Effects of Television, Video Games, and Computers.* Cambridge, MA: Harvard University Press, 1984.

> Greenfield believes that educators need to be aware of the benefits as well as the weaknesses of each medium in order to teach media literacy. Of particular interest is her final chapter, "Multimedia in Education," in which she concludes that media should be used in a variety of combinations to teach. She also believes that it is more effective to teach children about television at school than at home.

Herx, Henry, and T. Zaza, editors. *The Family Guide to Movies on Video: The Moral and Entertainment Values of 5,000 Movies on TV and Videocassette.* New York: Crossroad, 1988.

> This book features reviews of titles from the major studios and significant independent movies that are seen on broadcast and/or cable television or are available on video. Each short review (most are fewer than 100 words) includes information about the moral dimension of the story and treatment, age suitability, and the artistic and entertainment quality of the program. After each entry is a rating symbol used by the U.S. Catholic Conference Department. These include A, for general patronage; A-II, for adults and adolescents; A-III, for adults; A-IV, for adults, with reservations (this refers to certain movies that are not morally offensive in themselves but that do require some analysis and explanation to avoid mistaken interpretations and false conclusions);

and O, for morally offensive. The MPAA ratings can be found in the Glossary.

Kaplan, Don. *Television and the Classroom.* White Plains, NY: Knowledge Industry Publications, 1986.

> This slender book includes chapters covering topics such as television and language arts, social issues, television stereotypes, violence, and the news. Kaplan offers ideas that will enhance work with video activities.

Lacey, Richard. *Seeing with Feeling: Film in the Classroom.* Philadelphia: W. B. Saunders, 1972.

> Lacey is the creator of the "image-sound skim" (see Glossary). He is most concerned with helping students tap the feelings a film has evoked and was one of the first to see the value of short and feature films as a stimulus for thinking. In this book he offers many reflections and ideas for video-related activities to do with children.

Laybourne, Kit. *The Animation Book: A Complete Guide to Animated Filmmaking from Flip-Books to Sound Cartoons.* New York: Crown, 1979.

> This extensive resource offers information about many animators in the United States and Canada. It also gives step-by-step instructions on how to create several styles of animation, making the book a useful tool for teaching animation.

Laybourne, Kit, and P. Cianciolo, editors. *Doing the Media: A Portfolio of Activities, Ideas and Resources.* New York: McGraw-Hill, 1978.

> This anthology covers everything on teaching media—beginning with John Culkin's chapter "Doing the

Truth," which focuses on Marshall McLuhan's theory of the importance of seeing more, hearing more, and feeling more. The many contributors provide a wealth of information as well as engaging activities to help children become media literate. This volume is a must for anyone involved in a hands-on approach to media.

Lesser, Gerald S. *Children and Television: Lessons from Sesame Street.* New York: Vintage, 1974.

Lesser, who is educational director for "Sesame Street," has been involved with the landmark program since its inception. In this book he offers an inside look at how "Sesame Street" came to be and discusses both its successes and some of the criticisms it has received. Lesser has a thorough understanding of preschoolers that is backed by research. The text is very readable, and the doodles created by Maurice Sendak during "Sesame Street" production meetings add a wonderful touch of whimsy.

Maltin, Leonard. *Of Mice and Magic: A History of American Animated Cartoons.* New York: New American Library, 1980.

Beginning with Winsor McCay, Gertie the Dinosaur, and silent cartoons, Maltin's ambitious book fills a void by providing information about American cartoons and the people who created them. Through this book, which is sprinkled with wonderful pictures of the animators and their creations, readers will be drawn to consider this often-overlooked form of entertainment. Particularly useful for researchers and cartoon aficionados is a filmography by studio, listing all the cartoons and animated feature films by year.

Minton, Lynn. *Movie Guide for Puzzled Parents: TV, Cable, Videocassettes.* New York: Dell, 1984.

This guide includes more than 1,500 reviews of films rated G, PG, and R as well as listings of movies by both desirable categories (e.g., "good movies for all ages," "good movies for ages 9 or 10 and up," "worthwhile movies with a black hero or heroine") and undesirable ones (e.g., "movies that encourage speeding and bad driving").

Moody, Kate. *Growing Up on Television: A Report to Parents.* New York: McGraw-Hill, 1984.

In this thoughtful and useful book, Moody looks at the effects of television on children and suggests plans of action that can be taken in schools, in the home, and in society in general.

Mulay, James J., et al., editors. *Family Classics.* Chicago: CineBooks, 1988.

This well-researched book includes more than 450 reviews of films from the 1930s through *Who Framed Roger Rabbit?* Each review includes a description of the movie, a critical appraisal, and extensive production credits.

Palmer, Edward L. *Television and America's Children: A Crisis of Neglect.* New York: Oxford University Press, 1988.

Palmer is the former vice president for research at Children's Television Workshop. In this book he offers insights into who is to blame for the sad state of children's television. Citing statistics and anecdotes, he discusses how he thinks television could do what the public schools often don't do—teach children. Of particular interest is the chapter on the quality programming that is produced abroad.

Postman, Neil. *Amusing Ourselves to Death: Public Discourse in the Age of Show Business.* New York: Viking/Penguin, 1985.

> Postman's foreword compares prophecies made by George Orwell in *1984* and Aldous Huxley in *Brave New World*. Noting "man's infinite appetite for distractions," he says that "Orwell feared that what we hate will ruin us. Huxley feared that what we love will ruin us." Postman's book is about the possibility that Huxley, not Orwell, was right, and how this possibility relates to children and media.

Rice, Susan. *Films Kids Like: A Catalog of Short Films for Children.* Chicago: American Library Association, 1973.

> This slim book provides an annotated listing of excellent short films for young children.

Schickel, Richard. *The Disney Version: The Life, Times, Art and Commerce of Walt Disney.* New York: Simon & Schuster, 1985.

> Written by a noted film critic, this is an unauthorized biography offering a critical analysis of Disney's life and work, beginning with his birth in 1901.

Schneider, Cy. *Children's Television: The Art, the Business, and How It Works.* Chicago: NTC Business Books, 1987.

> Written by a veteran in children's television and the developer of Nickelodeon, the first cable network for children, this book offers invaluable information about the business end of "kidvid."

Singer, Dorothy G., Jerome Singer, and Diana Zuckerman. *Getting the Most Out of TV.* Santa Monica, CA: Goodyear, 1981.

> Recommended for use with students in third through sixth grades, this well-organized workbook offers work sheets for eight lessons: "The Technical Side of TV," "People Make Programs," "The Magic of TV," "The Characters We See on TV," "Action and Violence," "The Real World of TV," "Commercials," and "You and TV: Who's in Charge?" Background information is given for each unit and the sheets may be reproduced for classroom use. This book will be especially helpful for educators wanting to give students information about uses of the camera, special effects, and how television can manipulate the viewer.

Singer, Dorothy G., Jerome Singer, and Diana Zuckerman. *Teaching Television: How To Use TV to Your Child's Advantage.* New York: Dial, 1981.

> The authors of this book have done considerable research on the good and bad effects of television and feel that with guidance children can benefit from it. Chapters cover such topics as "how TV works" and "real and pretend." Each chapter includes a section on what the reader needs to know, a glossary of related words, and activities and discussion ideas. Also included are explanations about how children perceive television. This is a terrific book with many ideas to help children make sense of television.

Street, Douglas, editor. *Children's Novels and the Movies*. New York: Frederick Ungar, 1983.

Street looks at film adaptations of 24 children's classics (18 of which are available on video), including *Pinocchio, Kidnapped,* and *Island of the Blue Dolphins*. His extensive bibliography of selected titles will prove useful for students of children's film and video adaptation.

Thurber, Marshall, editor. *The Listening Road to Literacy: The Read-Along Handbook for Parents, Educators and Librarians*. Old Greenwich, CT: Literacy Publications, 1990.

This handbook is devoted to information about critical listening skills and activities using "read-alongs," books with audiotapes. Included are two sections of activities, one for children in kindergarten through third grade and one for fourth through sixth graders. Also included is a chapter on audiocassette repair.

Villalpando, Eleanor. *TV: A Tool To Turn on Thinking*. Phoenix, AZ: Think Ink, 1982.

Villalpando sees television as a resource and teaching tool. To that end, her workbook strives to prepare students to use television effectively. Topics covered include the sitcom, news, commercials, helping children become more discriminating viewers, cartoons, game shows, and sports shows. The work sheets, which are appropriate for children in the third grade and up, encourage students to predict, compare, analyze, discriminate, and evaluate. This excellent book includes many ideas for additional sheets, along with discussion topics.

Winn, Marie. *The Plug-in Drug: Television, Children, and the Family* (rev. ed.). New York: Penguin, 1985.

Winn is not a supporter of television. She assesses the long-term effects of the passive act of television watching and concludes that it is addictive, that it has a destructive effect on family life, that it decreases a person's motivation to read, that there is a negative relationship between television viewing and school achievement, that there is a strong link between television viewing and violence—and she goes on. Read her book and draw your own conclusions. Also look at some of her stories, which are available on video from the Learning Corporation of America or for the home market on the LCA label from New World.

Books about Children and Child Development

Briggs Myers, Isabel. *Gift Differing*. Palo Alto, CA: Consulting Psychologists Press, 1980.

This book describes the Myers Briggs Type Indicator, a testing instrument given adults. It is cited here because it gives a clear description of personality that is very helpful for understanding learning styles. Included is a chapter on learning styles that reinforces the idea that people receive information differently, an important concept for teachers to keep in mind when working with children.

Capacchione, Lucia. *The Creative Journal for Children: A Guide for Parents, Teachers, and Counselors*. Boston: Shambhala, 1989.

> This book offers 72 journal writing exercises to be used with children in kindergarten through junior high school. Each exercise comes with a descriptive name, procedure, purpose, and suggested uses. Many can be adapted to work with videos, and all will be useful for children who are involved in journal writing. This is an invaluable resource.

Healy, Jane M. *Endangered Minds: Why Our Children Don't Think*. New York: Simon & Schuster, 1990.

> Healy is a learning specialist who has taught at Cleveland State University and who is also a parent. In this book she puts forth a sound argument as to why children today are having difficulty with reading and critical thinking. Much of the book is based on recent research in neuropsychology (the investigation of the relationships among brain development, behavior, and learning). Healy regards the changes in contemporary life-styles and the influence of the electronic media, including television, video games, and computers, as causes of the problem. This readable book makes complex material accessible to the lay reader.

Healy, Jane M. *Your Child's Growing Mind: A Guide To Learning and Brain Development from Birth to Adolescence*. Garden City, NY: Doubleday, 1987.

> Filled with insights, suggestions, plans for action, and useful information, this book brings clarity to a field of study that is often perplexing—the brain. By helping readers to understand the child's brain and the way it develops, Healy helps them to understand how children learn.

Lickona, Thomas. *Raising Good Children*. New York: Bantam, 1983.

> This book is filled with invaluable information and hundreds of ideas to help foster moral development in children. Lickona looks at a child's moral growth as a developmental process. He clearly describes each age group and suggests ways of dealing with children as they grow through each phase of development. His chapter titled "Television as a Moral Teacher and What To Do about It" is excellent, providing frightening examples of what children learn from television, along with ideas for limiting viewing. Also included are four excellent appendixes: Appendix A examines the research behind moral development, Appendix B provides examples of ways to draw out a child's moral reasoning, Appendix C suggests using "Dear Abby" at the dinner table to stimulate discussions about morality, and Appendix D is an annotated list of books for children that foster moral values. Many of the books, fairy tales, and nursery rhymes listed have been adapted to video. This volume is highly recommended.

Oppenheim, Joanne, et al. *Choosing Books for Kids: How To Choose the Right Book for the Right Child at the Right Time*. New York: Ballantine, 1986.

> See the listing for this volume under "Books about Literature and Story," on p. 168.

Postman, Neil. *The Disappearance of Childhood*. New York: Delacorte, 1982.

In this compelling book, Postman documents the birth of the concept of childhood with the invention of the printing press and discusses the concept's evolution up to the present day. He believes that because of the electronic media, the concept of childhood is disappearing. This thoroughly researched and provocative book will cause readers to reconsider their understanding of the concept of childhood and to think hard about media's impact on children.

Winn, Marie. *Children without Childhood.* New York: Penguin, 1984.

Based on interviews conducted in two very diverse communities—Denver, Colorado, and Scotia, New York—Winn constructs an argument that children of the 1970s and 1980s are different from those who grew up prior to the 1970s. Winn documents that children today are more sophisticated and less protected than children in the past, a change she attributes to divorce and two-working-parent families.

Glossary

acting Performance of a role in a film, video, or dramatic production.

animation The cinematic process used to create the illusion of mobility through successive drawings of inanimate subjects.

camcorder A camera and videotape recorder combined in a single unit.

characters The people, animals, creatures, or monsters who have roles in books, films, or videos.

conflict Struggles or problems found in stories made into videos and films.

continuity The even flow of events in a dramatic production.

critical viewing skills The ability to analyze and evaluate what one sees and hears in all media.

counter A device on the VCR that counts seconds as the tape proceeds.

cue up Locate a specific point on the tape so that when "play" is pressed the tape will begin showing at that point.

director The person responsible for the overall quality of a production, including cinematic technique, actors' and actresses' performances, credibility, continuity, and dramatic elements.

here-and-now wheel A technique developed by Richard Lacey (*Seeing with Feeling: Films in the Classroom*, 1972) for identifying feelings at specific moments during a film or video program. Before watching a video, students draw a wheel with spokes. During the viewing they are periodically prompted by a teacher or discussion leader to note their feelings on specific spokes of the wheel. After the viewing the students discuss the feelings they identified at each point.

hero/heroine The central character or protagonist in a story, particularly in stories involving quests.

iconographic animation A camera technique used in photographing a page.

image-sound skim A technique developed by Richard Lacey (*Seeing with Feeling: Films in the Classroom*, 1972). In round-robin fashion, students recall the first image or sound that comes to mind when thinking of the film or video under discussion. Students continue contributing images and sounds until the topic is exhausted. Follow-up

178 Glossary

discussions adhere to the important points touched on during the image-sound skim.

intertitles Titles in a video or film that supply needed information, such as subtitles in foreign films or silent films.

laugh track Recorded laughter, often played on television situation comedies.

live action Photographing people, animals, and objects in motion for film or video versus animation photography.

media The various forms of mass communications, including newspaper, radio, television, computer, film, and video.

media literacy The ability to understand newspapers, radio, television, computers, video, and film. Media literacy is taught by encouraging children to focus on the acquisition of critical viewing skills through well-defined discussions and related activities.

MPAA ratings Ratings given by the Motion Picture Association of America to specify the appropriateness of a film's content for young audiences. Ratings are as follows: G, general audiences; PG, parental guidance suggested, some material may not be suitable for children; PG-13, parents are strongly cautioned to give special guidance for attendance of children under 13, some material may be inappropriate for young children; R, restricted, children under 17 require accompanying parent or adult guardian; NC-17, no children under 17 years of age admitted.

pantomime The acting out of a story or play without dialogue.

pathos An element in a film or video that causes the viewer to feel compassion or pity.

plot (1) The scheme or pattern of events and situations of a story (noun); (2) to plan a story, sequence by sequence (verb).

producer The person in charge of coordinating all of the activities connected with the production of a play, film, or radio, television, or video program.

production The overall process of making a film or video.

production values The quality of a film or video, including the camera work, lighting, direction of the actors and actresses, costumes, makeup, and set.

public performance rights The legal right to show a video to a group. Under federal copyright law, a video marked "Home Use Only" may be shown in a classroom or school library for the purposes of instruction, as long as the tape is a lawful copy.

script The material written for a stage, radio, film, television, or video program; includes the plot outline, brief descriptions of characters, settings, complete dialogue, narration, and limited descriptions of action and sound effects.

setting The time in history, time of year, time of day, and location in which a story takes place.

special effects Extraordinary effects beyond the capability of film or video that are inserted in the film by the special effects department after shooting.

story A written condensation of a narrative from which a script can be created; includes plot, conflict, characters, and setting.

storyboard Thorough sketches or photographs of planned shots, including dialogue, music, and sound effects indications, which are used as a guide for live-action and animated productions.

suspension of disbelief An audience's acceptance of what it sees in a television, film, or video story, however unlikely it may seem, such as accepting that animals are able to talk or that people are able to fly.

theme The principal idea or message of a film or video.

tragedy A drama in which the principal character or characters experience profound suffering and inner conflict, and that ends in death or disaster.

villain A wicked character in a story who opposes the hero or heroine.

Index

Abe Lincoln: Freedom Fighter, 87–88
Access, 6
Acting, 34–35, 37, 64–65
Action for Children's Television, 110
Activities. *See* Story comprehension activities; Video production activities; *specific activities*
The Adventures of Huckleberry Finn, 94
The Adventures of Milo and Otis, 96
The Adventures of Robin Hood, 27, 96
Age appropriateness, 6, 7, 83–84, 107–108
  fourth through sixth grade, 24–26, 27–28
  kindergarten through third grade, 20–24, 26–27
  parents' versus child's sense of, 110–111
  preschoolers, 19–20, 112–114
Almanac for Kids, 23
The American Film and Video Association, 8
American Graffiti, 26
American Library Association, 6
American Video Conference, 110
Animal ABCs, 21
Animal Alphabet, 21, 105
Animal Wonders from Down Under, 106
Animal Zoop, 105
Animals of Africa, 105, 106
Animation, classroom activities for, 36, 38, 65–66
Anne of Green Gables, 5, 88
Around the World with Cricket, 98
Art activities, 35–37
Ashpet 70, 97
Audiovisual librarian, educational function for, 3
The Author's Eye, 33
The Autobiography of Miss Jane Pittman, 27
Awards, 76, 109–110

Babar the Movie, 26
BabySongs, 112
Bank Street Read-Along Story Videos, 21
Be a Magician, 22
Beauty and the Beast, 26, 39, 40, 70, 103
"Ben's Dream," 23
The Bionic Bunny, 24, 42
The Birmingham International Educational Film Festival, 9
The Black Stallion, 91
Black-and-white videos, 12, 68–69
Bloom's classification system, 16–17

182   Index

Booklist, 8
Books, video activities with, 4, 33, 76–77
The Boy Who Could Fly, 91
Brown, Laurene K., 14
Buy Me That!, 102

Caldecott Medal, 76
California recommended reading list, 7
Camera operation, 41, 66–68
Chaplin, Charlie, 62
Characters
   activities for understanding, 30–31, 54–59, 88–89, 90–92
   heroes and villains, 58–59, 94–96
   interactions, 54
   motivation, 54–55
   personalities, 57–58
   students' feelings about, 56–57
Charlotte's Web, 4, 61
The Chicago International Festival of Children's Films, 9
Children's library room, 6
Children's Video Report, 7, 8
Choosing the Best in Children's Video, 70
CINE Golden Eagle, 109–110
City Lights, 62
Clay animation, 65
Cleary, Beverly, 21–22
Closed captions, 73–74, 100–102
Collage technique, 36
Color, 68–69
Comedy, 62–63
Comic strips, 67
Communication, 85, 99–100
Conflict, 31–32, 60
Corduroy and Other Bear Stories, 6, 19, 96, 97
Costumes, 39, 69
Counter, for VCR, 12–13, 99, 105
Counting, 21
The Cricket in Times Square, 95
Cricket's Clubhouse, 98

Critical viewing skills. *See* Media awareness
Curriculum Guide: Using Film and Video To Teach Writing and Critical Thinking, 9

Dance, 35
David Copperfield, 26
The Diary of Anne Frank, 27, 97
Diorama, 32, 60, 97
Discover Korea, 98
Discussion,
   facilitation of, 13–17
   leader, 78–79
   See also specific activities
Doing the Media, 38
Dr. Seuss stories, 21
Dramatization activities, 34–35
The Dream Is Alive, 27

Editing, 69
The Electric Grandmother, 5
The Elephant's Child, 40, 93, 94
Emotions. *See* Feelings
Encyclopedia Brown, 26
English as a second language, 73
Environmental awareness, 25
Ethnicity, 12
Evaluation of videos, 11–12
   awards, 109–110
   by children, 44, 45, 75, 81–84, 102–103
   film and video festivals, 8–9, 110
   by parents, 109–111
   reviews for, 7–8
   specific ages, 83–84
Evil characters, 59, 94
Exploring Books with Gifted Children, 16, 90

Faerie Tale Theatre, 114
Fahrenheit 451, 27
Fairy tales, 26
   conflict elements in, 60
   selection guidelines, 112–114
   in sign language, 99–100

value of, 111–112
visual imagery activity, 33
Family Circle Presents Storyland Theatre, 95
Fantasy stories, 25, 26, 27
Feelings
  kindergarten through third graders, 49
  preschool children, 20
  preteen children, 26, 77–78
  specific video program, 97–99
  about story characters, 56–57
Film Advisory Board, 110
Film and video festivals, 8–9, 110
First-grade children, 22
Flashbacks, 62
Flip books, 38, 65
Forced association questions, 17
Foreign language, 61
Fourth- through sixth-grade children, 24–26, 27–28
  exploring feelings, 77–78
  media awareness activities, 80–84, 102–103
  story comprehension activities, 51–63, 92
  thinking skills, 84–85
  video production activities, 63–75
"Freedom To View," 6
Frightening images, 20, 40
From Star Wars to Jedi: The Making of a Saga, 28
Fun in a Box 1, 23
Funding, 6

Geography, 25, 98
Get Ready, Get Set, Grow!, 22
"Getting To Know Maurice Sendak," 22
Gift of the Whales, 98
"The Gingerbread Man," 61
Goggles, 5
"Goldilocks and the Three Bears," 99–100

Hamlin, Marjorie, 16

Hansel and Gretel, 70
Happy Birthday, Moon and Other Stories, 114
Harold and the Purple Crayon, 31, 96
Hawk, I'm Your Brother, 26
Here We Go, 19
Heroes and heroines, 58–59, 95–96, 112–113
Hiroshima Maiden, 27
Hobbies, 23
The Hobbit, 54, 96
Hockey Night, 27, 91
Home Alone, 27
Home videos, 45
How the Camel Got His Hump, 93
How the Leopard Got His Spots, 93
Humor, 62–63
Hunter, Holly, 113–114

I Can Dance, 22
I'd Like To Teach the World To Sing, 98
Image-sound skim, 14–15, 33
In the Night Kitchen, 22
Inspirational stories, 27
Involvement questions, 17
Island of the Blue Dolphins, 25

Jack and the Dentist's Daughter, 70
Jacob Have I Loved, 27, 87, 89
Jim Henson's Play-Along Video series, 5
Journal writing, 79–80, 92–93
The Journey of Natty Gann, 57, 91
The Jungle Book, 61, 93

Kindergarten through third-grade children
  exploring feelings, 49
  listening skills development, 43–44
  media awareness activities, 44–46, 102–103
  media needs, 20–24, 26–27, 84
  story comprehension activities, 29–37, 90–91

Kindergarten through
    third-grade children
    (continued)
  thinking skills activities, 47–49
  video production activities,
    37–42

Lacey, Richard, 14
The Land of Faraway, 26, 91, 96
Language arts, 61, 79
  word appreciation activities,
    93–94
Lassie Come Home, 92
The Last Starfighter, 27
Library Journal, 8
Lifestyle, video's impact on, 83
A Link with Nature, 97
Listening skills development,
  43–44
Little League's Official How-To-Play Baseball by Video, 22
"Little Red Riding Hood," 99–100
Little Women, 54, 92
Look What I Made: Paper Playthings and Gifts, 27
Lyle, Lyle Crocodile: The Musical, 21, 27

Macmillan Video Almanac for Kids, 23
Madeline, 90
Make Way for Ducklings, 7
Man of the Trees, 24
The Man Who Would Be King, 26
The Maurice Sendak Library, 22, 96, 97
Media awareness
  fourth- through sixth-grade activities, 80–84
  kindergarten through third-grade activities, 44–46
  of parents, 107–110
  specific video activities,
    102–103
Media literacy, 180
Medicine Hat Stallion, 88
Meet Me in St. Louis, 27

Merlin and the Dragons, 94
"Mister Rogers' Neighborhood,"
  19, 111
Molly's Pilgrim, 7, 23, 98
Monterey Bay Aquarium, 23, 106
Movement activities, 35
Moyers, Bill, 58
Mrs. Frisby and the Rats of NIMH,
  61
Music activities, 35
Musical videos, 21, 27, 67–68
The Mysterious Tadpole and Other Stories, 95

National Captioning Institute, 100
The National Educational Film & Video Festival, 9, 110
The National Film & Video Market, 9
The National Soul: Myth, Morality, and Ethics in the American Consciousness, 58
National Velvet, 27, 92
Never Cry Wolf, 97
Newbery Award, 25, 76
Noah's Ark, 7, 39
Nursery rhymes, 32–33, 61
The Nutcracker: A Fantasy on Ice, 26
The Nutshell Kids, 22

Oliver! 94
Orchestra videos, 67–68
Out of Time, 26
Outlines, video activities for
  learning, 103–104

Pantomime, 34, 37
Parents, video evaluation by,
  109–111
Parents' Choice, 110
Pecos Bill, 110
Pinocchio, 20
Pippi Longstocking, 90
Plot, 30, 52–53, 89
Point of view, 63
Polette, Nancy, 16
Pollyanna, 90

Prejudice, 78
Preschool children
    media needs, 19–20, 107–108
    selecting videos for, 83–84,
        112–114
Pretending, separating from
    reality, 19–20, 48, 107–108
Previewing committees, 8
Production values, 39–40, 70
Public library, 4–5, 7–8
Publishers Weekly, 8
Puppets, 48

Quality of videos, 5
Quantity questions, 16
Quest stories, 96–97
Questions, for video discussion,
    13–17

*Raffi in Concert with the Rise and
    Shine Band*, 5
Raising Good Children, 26
Ramona series, 21–22, 26, 97
Reading, video activities with, 4,
    33, 76–77
"Reading Rainbow," 75
Really Rosie, 90
Red Riding Hood, 16
The Red Shoes, 27
Reorganization questions, 17
Research projects, 105–106
Reviews, 7–8
    by children, 44, 45, 75, 81–82,
        102–103
    publications for, 8, 110
    See also Evaluation of videos
*Richard Scarry's Best Alphabet
    Video Ever*, 21
*Richard Scarry's Best Counting
    Video Ever*, 21
The Right Stuff, 54
The Rotten Truth, 24

Sarah and the Squirrel, 97
Scenery, 39, 69
*Scholastic Blue Ribbon Storybook
    Video*, 96

School Library Journal, 8
Science, 46, 84
Science fiction, 25, 84
Scripting, 40, 70–71
Second-grade children, 22–23
*Seeing with Feeling: Films in the
    Classroom*, 14
Selection guidelines. See
    Evaluation of videos
Sendak, Maurice, 22, 84–85
Sensory information, 63
"Sesame Street," 19, 100
Setting, 31, 39, 59–60, 90
Sharapan, Hedda, 19
Show and tell, 45
Sign language, 99–100
Sign Me a Story, 99–100
16mm activities, 38, 49, 66
Smile for Auntie and Other Stories,
    7
Social studies, 46–47, 84, 98
Sometimes I Wonder, 22–23
Sound, in video production,
    41–42, 71–72
Special effects, 42, 72–73
Sports, 22
Star Wars, 25
Starlight Hotel, 57, 91
The Steadfast Tin Soldier, 110
Stereotypes, 47, 78
Storage, 6
Stories To Remember series, 39, 70
*The Story about Ping and Other
    Stories*, 21, 90, 96
Story comprehension activities
    book and video comparisons, 33
    dramatization, 34–35
    fourth through sixth grade,
        51–63, 87–92
    kindergarten through third
        grade, 29–37, 90–91
    specific video program, 87–92
    story elements, 30–32, 51–63
    visual imagery, 32–33
    See also specific story elements
Storyboarding, 40–41, 70–71
Storytelling, 46

Subtitles, 73–74, 100–102
Supposition questions, 17
Surveys, 44
Sweet 15, 25

Taking Advantage of the Media, 14
Teach Me To Dance, 5
Telephone game, 43
Television programs, 19, 81
Theme, 60, 89
"The Three Little Pigs," 113–114
Thinking skills activities, 47–49, 84–86
Third-grade children, 23
Three Billy Goats Gruff/The Three Little Pigs, 113
Three Richard Scarry Animal Nursery Tales, 113
Thumbelina, 95
Tommy Tricker and the Stamp Traveller, 27
Trade shows, 9–10
Tragedy, 61–62
Treasure Island, 61, 94
Tuchman, Barbara, 58
Tuck Everlasting, 25, 61, 88, 91, 92

Values, 78
VCR. *See* Videocassette recorder
The Velveteen Rabbit, 31, 40, 110
Vermont Department of Libraries, 5
The Video Guide to Stamp Collecting, 23
Video collection
  age guidelines, 6
  for classroom, 4
  conceptualization of, 5–6
  evaluation of videos for, 7–10
  for public library, 4–5
Video journal, 80, 92–93
The Video Letter from Japan, 25
Video Librarian, 8
Video production activities, 74–75
  acting, 37, 64–65
  animation, 38, 65–66
  camera work, 41, 66–68
  costumes/scenery, 39, 69
  editing, 69
  fourth through sixth grade, 63–75
  kindergarten through third grade, 37–42
  production values, 39–40, 70
  scripting/storyboarding, 40–41, 70–71
  sound, 41–42, 71–72
  special effects, 42, 72–73
"Video Rainbow," 75
Video Rating Guide for Libraries, 8
Video Review, 110
Videocassette recorder (VCR)
  counter for, 12–13, 105
  operation instruction, 74
  pervasiveness of, 3
Viewpoint questions, 17
Villains, 59, 94, 112–113
Violence, 62
Visual imagery, 32–33, 107–108
Vocabulary building, 43, 93

Walking on Air, 7, 27, 96
What's a Good Story? Beauty and the Beast, 39, 70, 103
What's Happening to Me?, 28
Where in the World: Kids Explore Kenya, 105
Where the Wild Things Are, 22, 96, 97
Who's Afraid of Opera?, 27
The Wind in the Willows, 95
The Wizard of Oz, 94
WonderWorks series, 91, 92
Woods, Frank, 5
Word appreciation, 93–94
A World Alive, 23, 27, 106
The World of Anne Frank, 27
The World of Ideas, 58
Writing activities, 15, 79–80, 92–93

You Can Choose series, 28
The Young Magician, 91

Zoom effects, 66, 67

Martha Dewing taught children ages three through eleven in independent schools in the United States and Austria for many years. She received a master of education in children's media from Harvard University. She has written video reviews for major publications across the country and serves on the editorial board for *Video Rating Guide for Libraries*. Her book, *Home Video in Libraries: How Libraries Buy and Circulate Pre-Recorded Home Video* was published in 1988 by G. K. Hall. Dewing lives in Princeton, New Jersey, and is editor of *Children's Video Report*, a newsletter focusing on children and video.